WHEN THE ROAD GETS ROUGH

WHEN THE ROAD GETS ROUGH

GETS ROUGH

NORMAN C. HILL

BOOKCRAFT
SALT LAKE CITY, UTAH

Library of Congress Catalog Card Number: 85-73653
ISBN 0-88494-592-8

3rd Printing, 1987

Printed in the United States of America

In many of the stories included in this volume, names and locations of people involved have been changed to maintain their preferred anonymity.

Contents

1

Adversity: Prologue to Discovery

We are all on a road going somewhere, a road marked by hopes, dreams, goals, and aspirations to be happy and successful. But the road ahead isn't always clear. When unexpected obstacles arise, we can often go around or over them; they can even provide additional incentive to achieve our cherished goals or to realize our best dreams. Sometimes, however, the obstacles are so great that we are forced to map out a new route to our destination, to review where we are going and how we will get there.

This book is about such detours in the lives of faithful Latter-day Saints. It is about hopes and wishes, joys and fears, ordinary lives pulled off course by unexpected and apparently needless misfortune: the fatal illness of a promising young doctor, the accidental death of a child, the extended unemployment of a business executive. These and other problems are explored candidly by good, faithful people who had anticipated the best of life, but who learned instead to deal positively with whatever came their way. Despite vibrant testimonies of the restored gospel, they have not found it easy to cope with their burden of trials. Some have stumbled under the weight, but each has come to terms with it. Some feel that they have grown and become better traveling their particular detour. Others simply note that their lives are now different, regretting opportunities lost but building a future on opportunities gained.

How do we deal with the difficulties of life? Are they tests of faith? trials of our willingness to obey the Lord? lessons to give us experience? punishments for sin? incentives to pursue righteousness? If we live long enough and care about enough people, we ask such questions. We want to know why bad things happen to good people. We want to know how to turn away from the anger, sadness, or cynicism of misfortune and turn instead to hope, faith, and trust in God. But how?

Ultimately, we will derive a personal answer to this question from our own experience, but these stories may help us to see roadblocks and detours as a natural part of living. As Elder Rex E. Pinegar noted in quoting C. S. Lewis: "The great thing, if one can, is to stop regarding all the unpleasant things as interruptions in one's 'own' or 'real' life. The truth is, of course, that what one regards as interruptions are precisely one's real life." (*They Stand Together: The Letters of C. S. Lewis to Arthur Greeves*, ed. Walter Hooper [London: Collins, 1979], p. 499; as quoted in *Ensign*, November 1982, p. 24.)

Our trials focus our attention on who we really are and what priorities we are pursuing. A handicapped child or chronically ill spouse may take extraordinary time and energy away from our trip up the freeway of success. Paradoxically, as we work through and fully come to terms with our feelings, our introspection and self-examination may draw us closer to the Lord. God is not at the top of the ladder of success: His way, His path lies elsewhere. Once we re-orient the course of our lives, our burden may indeed become light, the yoke possible to carry.

But why do some individuals draw strength from problems, continuing to pursue eternal life, while others falter and lose their way? How can we learn to cope? To whom can we go for help?

These are not easy questions, and the answers may be as varied as the people who ask them. But insights from the experience of others can help us to cope with our own difficulties. Elder Orson F. Whitney noted: "To whom do we look, in days of grief and disaster, for help and consolation? . . . [Those] men and women who have suffered, and out of their experience in suffering [have brought] forth the riches of their sympathy and condolences as a blessing to those now in need. Could they do this had they not suffered themselves?" (*Improvement Era,* November 1918.)

We often find it difficult to talk to others about our problems: we want to be pleasant company, to avoid explaining or justifying our difficulties. And others may find it difficult to listen, not knowing how to respond appropriately. Yet "talking it out" may be the best source of help. Sometimes, when we are troubled the most, mere advice is what we need the least. Perhaps a story will illustrate this best. A little boy was sent on an errand by his mother and took longer than expected. When he returned, his mother questioned him about the delay.

"I met another boy whose tricycle was broken and who was crying because he couldn't fix it. So I helped him," the boy replied.

"But you don't know how to fix a tricycle," his mother said curiously.

"No, I don't. So I sat down and cried with him," he said.

There are many things that can't be fixed. Consolation helps. Faith helps. God helps. He has promised never to forsake us, never to leave us alone. After the Prophet Joseph Smith had erred once, the Lord lovingly reproved him: "Yet you should have been faithful; and he would have extended his arm and supported you against all the fiery darts of the adversary; and he would have been with you in every time of trouble" (D&C 3:8).

There once was a son who was estranged from his father and moved as far away from him as he could. After long years of separation, his anger seeped away. He wrote to his father about getting together and reconciling their differences. His father welcomed the opportunity and asked his son to return home. The son said he would not travel that far. His father's reply? "Come as far as you can; I will travel the rest of the way." So it is with God, our Heavenly Father. When our faith falters, when our burdens seem too much to bear, when life seems unfair and not at all what we deserve, we need only turn to Him. He will come the rest of the way.

The stories in this book may help us to retain faith and hope when things go wrong.

2

Yes, Divorced

I grew up in a small town in Utah with a century of Church tradition and family ties in our ward. Active in the Church throughout my youth, I was deacons and teachers quorum president, priests quorum secretary, Eagle Scout, full-time missionary, and at college, the ward clerk. I attended Brigham Young University on an academic scholarship and looked forward to a promising future in one of several fields that interested me.

A few months before I began at BYU, Kaye first heard about the Church and joined it. While her family allowed this action, they were not interested in the Church themselves. She also came to BYU on an academic scholarship to complete her education and to learn about the gospel more completely. I met her early in my senior year at BYU while sitting next to her in a religion class. It didn't take long from there. Three months later, after my graduation, we married in the temple. We left immediately to begin my Ph.D. program and finish her baccalaureate program at an eastern university.

By all appearances, we had an ideal marriage. She was bright and attractive, I was a promising graduate student. We loved each other, communicated well, and were very happy when we were together. We talked about the marriage problems of other graduate student friends and felt that we were happier and better adjusted than anyone we knew.

Then one Sunday about midway through my first year of graduate school it happened. I can still remember it clearly though it was almost sixteen years ago. We were driving home from a testimony meeting when Kaye turned to me and said: "It's not true, I don't believe it the way they do. I can't go back to the Mormon church again. If any church is true it is my parents' church and not yours."

I was shocked. What in the world was she saying? She couldn't be serious? But she was. Looking back there were small signs I might have seen . . . a complaint about my being called as a scoutmaster and the time it took, a reluctance to read the scriptures, and her hesitance about accepting a calling. But I had not noticed them at the time and now I was at a total loss for words. When we arrived home I didn't know how to respond. I couldn't believe this was happening. But it was. We prayed and talked the rest of the day and most of the night. Gradually I began to understand what she was really saying. She had been attracted to the fruits of Mormonism—the ideals and promises—but now, more than two years later, she realized the personal sacrifice required. She really didn't want that much imposition on her life, didn't want to leave the traditions of her parents, and didn't believe they could have been wrong all those years. Sadly, she was more attracted to the intellectual ideas our professors and fellow students were presenting than to the simplicity of the gospel. She felt that the local LDS church leaders and our LDS friends were narrow-minded and tradition-bound and could not possibly be inspired. Her parents' more humanistic church traditions were more compatible with modern times, she said.

During the next few weeks and months we had some long and concentrated discussions. We agreed on several things: we loved each other and we wanted children. But she did not want them to be raised in the gospel and I was not interested in any other way. So we decided that we would spend the next year or two trying to come to an agreement about the Church before starting a family.

At the end of two years of patient and intense effort on both our parts, she was more convinced than ever (with her parents' encouragement) that the Church was out of step with the times, while I was more convinced than ever that it had never been more relevant. We both recognized that life-long conflicts about the things we held most precious would be intolerable. So after earnest prayers and frequent discussions with the bishop and my father, I asked her for and eventually obtained a cancellation of our temple sealing.

While I had had feelings of impending doom for several months before the divorce was granted, I had two distinctly different feelings following it. The first was freedom from being forced to walk in a direction I knew was wrong and I didn't want to go. It was a deep sense of relief . . . I could start again. The second was a profound feeling of loss of a future. While young, I had dreamed about being different things when I grew up, like a doctor or a policeman. But most of all, I had dreamed about being an ideal Mormon father and having a happy family. That's why I had chosen sociology with an emphasis on family relations for my degree. While I was married there was still some hope for realizing my ideals. Now all that seemed lost. I was convinced that I had made the right decision for me in asking for a divorce, since we had no children and our differences were so irreconcilable. I felt certain that the decision was necessary and correct. But I felt now that I would never be able to find a faithful LDS woman who would consider me. I felt cut off forever from the joys of family life. Further, I felt my faith in the Church would always be suspect and my service offerings unwelcome. I felt that I had stigmatized myself for the rest of my life because I was a "divorcee." I tried to console myself by thinking, "If I am personally lost to the celestial kingdom, at least I can help others by encouraging them."

Despite such resolve, going to church was a chore to be endured each week. Talks seemed to focus constantly on family, the evils of divorce, or similar topics. I felt singled out. An object lesson to all who spoke. I knew I was being hypersensitive but it was difficult during those days to ignore my own feelings of unworthiness, of not fitting in, of being in the right church but on the wrong pew. I went to church, not for strength or support, but because I knew it was where I should be on Sunday. Since I had sought a divorce because of my faith in the gospel, how could I then reject it? I didn't fit in but I wasn't going to be left out.

Many of the ward members were shocked when they heard the news of my divorce. We had seemed happy together. What was the problem? Why couldn't we work things out together? Many were kind and sincerely helpful. But I didn't want to be catered to, I didn't need fellowshipping. I was irritated by good intentions which only seemed to reinforce my self-doubts. "If I didn't have a problem, why were so many people trying to help me?" I wondered. I resisted such feelings. I wasn't bad, I told myself. I wanted others to see that my life had been moving in a wrong and unhappy direction . . . tied to a daily disappointment and conflict over the things I held most dear. Now I was starting in the right direction again. But I didn't know how to say that to others in a way that made sense. I knew the tune but not the words to the music.

Immediately following my divorce, there were physical arrangements to be made, a house trailer to be sold, possessions and memories to be sorted and divided, and always the pressure of school. But there was also time to brood, to feel sorry for myself. Why had I, the good church boy, been fooled into marrying a closet doubter? I thought I was inspired in asking her to marry me. Was I wrong? What about other times when I felt inspired? Was I wrong then, too? I wanted to hate Kaye for destroying my dreams. But how could I hate her for openly communicating her deepest feelings? Gradually, my feelings of anger turned to sadness that such a good person had made such a bad use of her own agency, that she was influenced more by her parents and peer group than by the Spirit of the Lord.

I was at a low ebb in the subsequent weeks and months. Because I believed that others were judging me negatively, I found my personality changing despite my best efforts. My normal positive, outgoing personality became withdrawn and negative. I developed a stutter. I had difficulty meeting people and making friends. I was going to pieces.

I immersed myself in my graduate program, arriving at school early each day and staying as late as possible. Perhaps through hard work and focusing on other things, I could stop feeling self-pity and get on with my life. Working hard left less time to dwell on my problems, but it didn't change how I felt about myself or my situation.

While we were married, I used to fall back on Kaye in social situations. If we spent the evening with another couple whom I did not particularly like, I relied on my wife. When I no longer had a wife, I didn't know how to act. I had to learn social etiquette and other things all over again.

It was difficult for me to feel comfortable with the friends Kaye and I had developed together. Without her, I felt out of place with them. They were our friends as a couple and many of them were at a loss as to how to relate to me alone. Rightly or wrongly, I felt that the wives were all thinking:

"What has he done to that poor woman? Is he chasing after someone else?" Most of the men were sympathetic. Some had known about my struggle to teach and let the Spirit convert my wife. Some had fasted and prayed with me or had made special efforts to fellowship Kaye. But they still felt awkward at having a single friend in their home and conversations were often uncomfortable. I felt awkward, too.

Two particular families kept me going. The first was a young couple with two children who just liked me as a person and were able to continue to enjoy being friends with me. I visited them one night a week for about a year. We watched TV or chatted or played with their children. It was easy to feel that they were having fun with me as an individual and not as a divorced person. The other family was an older couple with no children at home. The husband had recently joined the Church. We enjoyed discussing the gospel together and talking about important values. Such association helped me relate to others even when I felt miserable and just wanted to be left alone. They always seemed to invite me to go places with them—especially ward social activities—in a way that I knew they wanted *me*. They weren't fellowshipping me, they enjoyed my company and I liked theirs.

In the midst of working through this personal turmoil, I received a phone call from the bishop. When we met, he extended a call to serve as a stake missionary. "Me? You want me?" I remember asking. How could a person who was divorced preach the family-centered gospel? Despite the bishop's confidence in me, I lacked confidence in myself. Although I didn't think it was the right calling for me, I accepted it anyway. As time passed, however, I found it gave me something to talk to other ward members about without being self-conscious. I had a reason for being at church and had something specific to do. There was a place for me after all. By reaching out to others, I changed.

In time I gave up my need to feel lonely. I gave up some

of those painful memories that seemed to torment me, and my resentment toward others lessened and then fell away. I progressed through three stages to a higher plane of acceptance of myself and others: Level One—"Boy, am I a rotten person"; Level Two—"Even if I am a rotten person, I am still better than *you are*"; Level Three—"I'm making progress and so are you." What had made the difference? Why did I change? I don't know for sure. Why does anyone change, really? I suspect that I was tired of feeling sorry for myself. Tired, especially, of trying to justify those negative feelings to someone else. It's much harder to feel persecuted when one has to explain it continually to someone else.

Three years after the divorce, I met the sister of a friend and quickly fell in love. A convert, she seemed "right" for me in so many ways. But through our months of courtship, I was constantly plagued with fears that some day she might lose her testimony. Several times, I almost stopped seeing her. Maybe I was born to be a loner. The old self-doubts returned again. I tried to talk to her about it. She startled me when she had some doubts about *my* steadfastness in the gospel. "If you think you're invulnerable, you're too cocky for me. Without humility, no one can handle life's common, everyday, garden-variety difficulties."

Shortly afterward, we were married in the Logan Temple. My stuttering soon stopped and I overcame other self-conscious habits I had developed.

Since that time, as a bishop, a branch president, and a friend, I have known many people who have gone through the traumatic experience of divorce. Some are filled with guilt; some worry about mistakes they think they made; some are relieved and feel a new sense of hope; some become withdrawn and sullen. They cannot be treated as members of a category to which a standardized response will always be helpful. Each needs to be recognized as a person and related to as any other person with love, friendship, and trust.

As human beings, we fortify ourselves in many different

ways when faced with a difficult situation. Numbness, silence, inattention, and suspicion are only a few of the materials out of which our personalities construct walls. To try to scale such walls—to "help" someone else—is arrogance; to fail to try is unforgivable. We may fail to reach them because of our clumsiness or the height of the walls, but we must try. Perhaps inviting them out of their stronghold might work just as well as attempting to batter down their walls. Inside the strongest citadel that a person can construct, he awaits his besieger.

I don't talk about having a divorce very often, because I don't see much use to it. Sometimes when I do I know the scar is not totally gone. I remember a conversation with our Relief Society president, herself divorced years ago, who had a granddaughter visiting her. She related that this young child had turned to her with tear-filled eyes and said, "Grandma, I'm going to be sad that you won't be with us in heaven." "What do you mean, sugar?" she had asked. "Well, divorced people can't go to heaven you know," the young girl replied. "My friend told me so." "Don't worry dear child," she responded, "divorce is only a word used on earth. If I live right, it won't matter in heaven."

Old prejudices die hard . . . both mine and others. But they don't last forever.

3

My Son Was Kidnapped

The stake president called in the early afternoon. He asked if he and his wife could come over about 6:00 P.M. Would Bea and I both be home? "Sure," I said, "no problem." But as I phoned my wife, I wondered about the call. Why would the stake president make an appointment and bring his wife? I had been stake president myself for fourteen years and had never taken my wife with me to an appointment in a member's home, so it couldn't be a stake calling. What, then? When I phoned my wife and told her about the call, she, too, speculated about the reason for the visit. Suddenly, her voice on the other end of the phone faltered, "It's Thayne," she said, "something's wrong with Thayne. I just know it." Thayne, our youngest son, was nearing the end of his mission in Argentina. "I'm sure that's not it," I tried to reassure her, but I had a strange sense of foreboding that made my words sound hollow even to me.

When the stake president and his wife arrived, we chatted for a few moments and then he came right to the point. My stomach tightened. "Your son has been kidnapped by a terrorist group. I had a call from Salt Lake City earlier today. The terrorists want money, a million dollars, before they'll release Thayne and his companion."

I couldn't move. I felt a gnawing pit in my stomach. I worked for an import-export company and knew Central and South America quite well. Our family had even lived in Panama for three years. I knew that terrorist groups were a way of life in many countries. They wanted a million dollars, but then what? Paying a ransom seldom resulted in the release of a victim. I knew that from experience. So now what? What do we do now?

It was a night I'll never forget as long as I live regardless of how long that is. I only hope that if I am not allowed to live to see my parents again that someone will discover this journal I am keeping and give it to them. I know it will comfort my mother.

We had taken the bus to meet some investigators. They met us at the bus stop in a car and drove us toward their home. Suddenly, the car stopped on a deserted street and four men with weapons appeared from nowhere. One began poking me with a knife and ordered us out of the car. When we were in the street, the car sped off. We were taken into the woods, blindfolded, our hands tied behind our backs, and walked in circles several times so we would not know the direction we were going.

We walked a long distance that night. I don't know how far it was but it took us all night: through the woods, a swamp, back in the woods again was all I could tell through the blindfold. Then, we were put in a small boat to cross a river. A storm came up as we were crossing and the boat began taking on water. I threw off my overcoat and untied my hands and blindfold, but before I could help my companion escape, I was grabbed from behind and held fast. When we reached shore, we were taken into the jungle to a prearranged spot. Our captors went into a small building on the edge of a clearing while we were taken by a guard to a hand-dug pit in the ground a few feet away. The pit had about twenty-five gunny sacks for a floor and a vine-tied covering for a roof. Cold and shivering, we were given some civilian clothes and two blankets. We changed, except for our garments. We didn't care how cold our wet garments made us feel, no one could make us take them off. So here we sit, who knows where, not knowing what tomorrow will bring. Trusting in the Lord that somehow we will be able to come out of this all right.

We didn't sleep much that night, we were so worried about Thayne. We felt so helpless. We were so far away. We knelt and prayed for the longest time. The words of temple covenants came into my mind. Was I willing to consecrate everything that the Lord had given me in building His Kingdom? Yes, I had made that commitment. But it was *my* life, *my* time, not my son's. He had so much to live for, so much to look forward to. *Take me instead. Dear Lord, let me trade places with him.*

The next morning we flew to Salt Lake City so that we would be able to discuss Thayne's situation on a direct basis with Church officials. We met with Elder McConkie and discussed the ransom note. "You can't pay it," I told him. "It won't do any good; even if you do, they won't let him go. He may not even be alive now. It would endanger missionaries everywhere." My wife burst into tears, sobbing uncontrollably. We were prepared for the worst, but it seemed that saying it out loud made it all the more ominous. We had prayed to the Lord and knew that no ransom could be paid. We felt we were signing a death warrant. Elder McConkie indicated that after prayerful consideration, the First Presidency reluctantly felt the same way. No ransom would be paid.

When I awoke after the first night in the pit, fright grabbed me. What were we going to do? What did they want with us? How long were they going to force us to live this way? Elder Shaw and I prayed more fervently than we have ever prayed. Tearful and trembling, we called upon Almighty God in the heavens to deliver us. The sweetest thought then occurred: many people will be praying for us once our abduction is discovered. Dad and Mom, my brothers and their wives, President Fernandez, the other missionaries, the prophet and other General Authorities. Praying for us, so many good people concerned about me. I was overwhelmed with the thought and told my companion about this impression. Solemnly, he said he had just had the same exact impression. At that instant, we knew that we were in the Lord's care. Even if we were killed, it would be for His own purpose.

I can't sleep very well at night and so I often end up pacing the hallway. Sometimes I walk outdoors just to look up at the star-filled sky. I used to stare into the night and gaze at the vastness of space. Doing so made me feel that God was in the heavens watching over all of his creations and protecting them. I don't feel that way tonight. Now, I walk outside to plead with Him to protect my son. "Please, dear God, please. Don't let this happen to me. Don't let our son disappear without a trace."

I strain hard to listen. I stay on my knees believing the Lord will answer my prayer. I have nowhere else to go, no place else to turn. There is absolutely nothing I can do but rely upon Him. I feel absolutely helpless. I want to do something, anything. But there is nothing I can do. Nothing but wait.

The rain stopped yesterday. It has been so cold each night that we welcome each new day for the sunshine it brings despite our uncertainty about our future. Today, the third day of our captivity, we have been given a hymn book and a pamphlet about Joseph Smith that was saved when the boat capsized. We were so grateful for it and spent most of the day in a devotional. Elder Shaw and I talked about the value of this capture in making us humble, prayerful, and dependent on the Lord. We bore our testimonies to each other again and again and promised we would not deny our faith regardless of what these men might do to us.

Each day passes so agonizingly slow for Bea and me. What can we do? Nothing. So we wait. And pray. And hope. The nights are worse. We stay up as long as we can because each night Bea has a frightening recurring dream: our son is a baby again, sleeping quietly in his crib. Suddenly from nowhere, a stranger comes and takes him. But he can't find his way out of the house. He's trapped. So he hides. Bea runs frantically, desperately through each room of the house. But she cannot find him. The dream plays over and over unmercifully.

Bea is given a blessing by President Romney. "We don't know whether your son is alive or not," he says, "but we feel good about it." We cling to such hope. President Romney is most concerned about us: will we become bitter, resentful if our son does not return from his mission? We assure him we won't. But later that night, we talk about it. What if we never hear from or see Thayne again? What if he just disappears without a trace? How will we react? We try to talk about it, but it's difficult. We want to hope for the best, but we don't want to create false expectations. We want to be prepared regardless of the outcome.

It's been so cold again. Night after night. We have thought of escape, but to what? We don't know where we are. The jungle is all around us. Even if we could overpower the one guard who watches us, where would we go? So instead of force, we've tried kindness. We gave a guard who was coughing last night an overcoat to protect him against the bitter cold. Then, today, he returned the favor. He let us out of the pit to stretch our legs.

Finally! It feels so good just to walk. Such a little thing I had always taken for granted before.

We search the scriptures each morning looking for help to pull us through this ordeal. We are buoyed temporarily by the words we read, only to talk ourselves out of expecting too much. Are we expecting too little? Are we limiting the Lord by not having hope? We want to believe that, as with Abraham, God will intervene at the last possible moment and deliver our son and his companion. But who are we to counsel God? To tell Him when to intervene and on what terms? My own words of counsel a few weeks ago to a troubled young couple came back to me. Mockingly, it seems. Could I take my own advice? Could I accept the Lord on His terms and not mine? Can I adjust to conditions that are unexpected and unwanted? Or would I sulk when things did not go my way? Now that I was on the receiving end, could I accept my own words as more than abstract concepts?

I want to believe. *Help me, dear Lord. Help Thou my unbelief.*

This morning Bea read this scripture to me: ". . . but we glory in tribulations also: knowing that tribulation worketh patience; And patience, experience; and experience, hope; And hope maketh not ashamed; because the love of God is shed abroad in our hearts by the Holy Ghost which is given unto us." (Romans 5:3–5.)

Our captors took off their masks today and began treating us poorly—yelling at us when we were let out of our pit to exercise and occasionally shoving us to get out of their way. Each day I write I wonder if it will be my last, wonder if this notebook will ever be discovered. At least it gives me something to do.

Today is our fifth day of captivity. It is late in the evening, we have considered escape again because it appears that things are turning for the worst. We hear shooting and fighting in the guard's area. What is going on? Is this it? We lie quietly, then a flashlight is shown in our eyes.

"Get your hands up!" someone shouts. A man with a helmet wearing a poncho presses his rifle in my nose, ordering me not to say a word. Men are running all over the little clearing in the jungle. My companion, misunderstanding this order, stands up instead. A rifle discharges near me as I turn to look for my companion. He's been shot! He lies doubled over on the ground as my hands are tied behind my back. "Who are you?" I ask the man tying my hands together. "The police," he says. Oh, no, the police have shot Elder Shaw because they think he's one of the captors. I try to explain, to tell them who we really are, but no one will listen. I am told to stop talking, that everything will be straightened out at police headquarters, but not until then.

I have a new appreciation for the scripture that indicates we should "pray unceasingly." I just wish there was something I could *do*.

This agonizing event has caused us to evaluate our lives carefully. We've looked under a microscope at everything we are involved in. Some things which seemed pretty important two weeks ago don't seem to matter much now. Except for the people we love and care about, what else is there? Odd how such trite observations seem so profound.

We focus on things which matter to us. Each son has served a mission, each returned to marry in the temple. Such good boys, such noble sons, every one. Now, Thayne, our last, on a mission. Where else would we rather have him? What nobler cause? How could we ever be bitter? I thanked God that he lived a life worthy to serve a mission. We wanted nothing less than the best we could give each of our sons. A mission was the best we knew how to give them. If there was something better, we would give that. Sending our sons on missions was the best we knew.

After a couple of minutes, Elder Shaw rouses. He is in great pain. We are told that everyone would have to walk out of the jungle with their hands tied. My companion has already lost a lot of blood but struggles to his feet. After a few hundred yards, they finally untie our hands so I can help him walk. I put my arm under his right shoulder and drag him most of a mile. When the police stop to rest, Elder Shaw is so weak that he can hardly speak. He has lost a tremendous amount of blood. While holding him with my left hand, I place my right hand on his head and command him—through the power of the Holy Melchizedek Priesthood—to have sufficient strength until he can get to a doctor to be taken care of. When we started again, his step picked up. Though he walked with great difficulty, he walked. Later, Elder Shaw was told by a doctor who examined him that he had less than a pint of blood left in his body. After walking another mile, we reached a pickup truck which took Elder Shaw to the hospital.

How can I describe how I felt when I heard the news? They were alive! They were safe! The uncertainty and lonesome waiting of the days before vanished. Gone. What exquisite news. They were free!

I have wondered many times since how I would have reacted if my son had never come home. I would be saddened, to be certain. Each parent silently hopes all his children will live longer than he, I think. Even now, I do not have that assurance. There are no guarantees, even now. Like any parent, I want my children to have a fulness of life here and in the hereafter. A mission is such an important part of that fulness that I could only be grateful that my son was called to serve. What parent would want it any other way?

I'm a different person than I was before the kidnapping. I'll never be the same again. It may not be noticeable outwardly, but an avalanche has happened inside. I had prided myself in the past on being able to "face the worst" and, through hard work and self-determination, overcome it. After all, I had spearheaded construction of many church buildings in the South despite limited funds and local political opposition. I had prospered as a businessman despite repeated setbacks. I had raised three sons who all served missions despite living mostly in small branches with limited church membership. Despite such accomplishments, after all is said and done, I discovered that I can't always pick myself up by my bootstraps and change things which I don't like. I am vulnerable. My prayers, my relationship to the Lord, will never be the same again, either. It's not just gratitude I feel—although I have a debt of gratitude which I can never fully repay—it's a recognition of my dependence on the Lord. I can't go it alone. I can't do it by myself. I need Him. Regardless of events or how they may "turn out."

If I could have raised enough money to pay the ransom for my son's release, I would have done it. I had discussed this possibility with Church officials. If I took this action as a private individual, it would protect the Church and the missionary work. Would it have done any good? Probably they wouldn't have been released anyway, and I would have been saddled with an awful debt after raising such ransom money. That wouldn't have mattered, though. Any parent would do anything he could to save one of his children or grandchildren in such circumstances. But I was powerless to do anything myself. I *had* to rely on the Lord.

In the past ten years since Thayne's release, I've often thought about this ordeal. I'm grateful as a parent that he's home and well and pursuing worthy goals. But I have gained more than gratitude for his well-being from this experience. In countless ordinary circumstances, I have recognized my own inability to change some things. For some things, it takes trust and faith in God—especially when things don't turn the way I might want them.

4

First, You Cry

Here we are, Larry and I, two young parents suitable for framing. We have all the makings of a storybook family. Larry is an associate professor at the University of Arizona, the recipient of several prestigious fellowships and grants, and bishop of our ward. I have a degree in music, taught school several years in Boston, have just been released as Relief Society president, and have been blessed with four superb children. Home is a modest suburban house that, although not extravagant, is a nice place to begin—like landing on Marvin Gardens after the first roll of the dice when playing Monopoly. A few monopolies and some mortgages later, we expect to improve our situation, even if we don't land on Park Place.

But I worry about Steven. He is two and had what the doctors called a "mild case" of meningitis a year ago. I've worried about him ever since. I have never been a "worrier" so I am surprised at my own reaction. Perhaps because he is our youngest I feel this way.

I know it's not fair to compare, but I do. Steven seems to be behind all of the others at this same age. I know it is not right to push, but I can't seem to help it. "How old are you, Steven? Come on, sugar, I'll help you." I hold up two fingers. "How many fingers?" Steven just smiles.

He is like a stranger, a shy and serene bystander even at boisterous family reunions. He sits quietly at the dinner table, too—"Off in his own world," I tell myself. I worry that he is not smart.

I have felt very tired lately and so I began taking vitamin and iron supplements. I try to convince myself that I'll begin to feel better after a few weeks, but I am not very convincing. I feel as if I'm moving in slow motion. By eleven o'clock in the morning, I feel like taking a nap.

My visiting teachers have just arrived. I've enjoyed them as much as any visiting teachers I've had. We talk about our families, the neighborhood, the teachers at school, and they give their message. A neighbor drops by and wants to talk about a play the second graders are planning to do and asks if I'll do the choreography for it. I want to be her friend and to be involved at school and so I agree. She continues to stay and visit, but I notice that it is almost time to begin dinner and I have housework to do. She finally leaves and I try to catch up on the things which need to be done.

I can't find Steven. Frantically, I run through the house looking for him. I hear the water running in the upstairs bathroom and burst through the door to find him fully clothed playing in the bathtub with the water running. He is oblivious to my presence, with his back to me even though I am loudly scolding him.

Dr. Huffman has asked both Larry and me to come to his office for our follow-up visit after Steven's latest physical examination. Dr. Huffman is a specialist whom we have been referred to by our regular pediatrician. "Your son has sustained some brain damage as a result of the meningitis. It's hard to tell how much for certain because he has a major hearing loss. He is almost functionally deaf." We discuss some details and agree to further tests before fumbling to the car and driving home.

Larry and I pray together that night as always. But it is an insincere prayer. We don't talk to the Lord or each other about Steven. We pretend. Things will be all right in the morning, I tell myself. We will probably get a call from Dr. Huffman telling us that there's been a big mistake, someone mixed up Steven's test results with another boy's and everything's all right after all. But I can't even convince myself.

We lie beside each other, side by side, no longer feeling young. I hear a tiny little voice, the boo-hooing of a sweet little child whose scoop of ice cream has just fallen from the top of his cone. It is the sound of despair that I have heard many times from one of my children before saying, "Don't worry, honey, Mommy will buy you another one. There's nothing to worry about. Don't cry." Such words have always provided miraculous consolation. Only it is not a child who is crying this time, it is me. How am I going to handle a child like this? Other people have handicapped children, not me. I never even felt comfortable around people who had obvious disabilities. I didn't know what to do or say. Now I have a child who cannot hear and may not be able to learn. What am I going to do? I feel beyond the reach of anyone's capacity ever to "make it all better."

In the weeks and months which followed our conversation with Dr. Huffman, it seemed that tensions and arguments between the children were always just around the corner. Someone was forever spilling his milk at the dinner table or leaving toys out to be run over by a car backing out of the driveway. Friction erupted between Larry and me as well. I resented the long hours he spent at the office or assisting ward members. I loathed Sundays and the loneli-

ness of sitting without a husband on the back row with four
children who seemed increasingly to misbehave.

I can't sleep very well at night and so I often get up and
stare into the fireplace. "Help!" I whimper. "I'm cracking
up." The moment I hear my words I know they are true.
Here, in the middle of the night when the rest of the house
is sleeping, is when I can hear myself think. I sit up, bring
my knees up to my chin, wrap my arms around my legs,
and try to keep my composure. Something's got to give. I
just can't do it all.

I have been angry at everyone lately, but especially resentful of Larry. It seems he will gladly help Sarah with her
homework or play with the older two boys, but never has
enough time left over for Steven. Or me. We haven't been
drifting apart, we are falling apart. So we have started seeing
a marriage counselor. Larry's embarrassed to do so. Others
have come to him for such advice. Will they ever again?

When I woke up this morning, I couldn't get out of bed.
Larry has a class to teach and is running late. I try to move,
but I just can't. All I can do is cry.

I had never known anyone who had ever had a nervous
breakdown before. Now I do. Me. I spent a week in the hospital recovering and then I was able to go home. My mother
came and stayed for some time and was a great help to me
in so many ways. I wanted someone just to take care of *me*
for a while. She does that better than anyone in the world. It
felt so good to have someone nurture me. She let me feel
sorry for myself without chastising or criticizing. Like a
public building, my facade is usually well kept. But there
are private, almost unexplored passages that I hardly realize
myself are there until I find a truly listening, nonjudgmental
ear.

After my mother left I said to myself, "Well, this is my
challenge and I've got to deal with it." Friends and neighbors helped form a safety net and assisted with ordinary
tasks in the ensuing few weeks. I tried "spring cleaning" for

both the house (moving furniture, buying things, throwing stuff away) and for me (planning, goal-setting, reflection). It was apparent that I was really going to have to work hard on some very basic things if life was not going to pass me by. I wasn't prepared for that part. I expected the planning and organizing would be the difficult part. Instead, I found that the challenge of living the routine, day-to-day parts of my life could be the most demanding. When the casserole dishes stopped coming from my neighbors, and the laundry started piling up, the "real world" began again.

Barbara, a neighbor, came over frequently in those early weeks. Ever wanting to be helpful and supportive, she was full of suggestions. "Make a schedule first thing in the morning and stick with it." "Block out some time for yourself." "Get out more and mingle; staying home makes anyone depressed." She seemed to have an endless repertoire of helpful comments. Though I knew she meant well, I was always relieved when she left. Her most common admonition was "not to worry." "Easy for you to say," I thought. Such advice is not very helpful unless it is followed by *because*. Being told not to worry seemed to me to be a way of saying, "Let's keep things superficial. I don't want to be bothered with working through your real problem."

The hardest part of my re-entry was the feeling I had that others were walking on eggs when they were around me. I felt labeled as "inadequate" because I had had a nervous breakdown. Instead of being given assignments at Relief Society or at PTA meetings, I was passed by. It was as if others were saying, "Oh, don't give her anything more to do. She can't cope with her family as it is."

A friend suggested that I try keeping a journal to record my deepest feelings and perhaps thereby work through them better. It didn't help me. It seemed so much like an obligation—like scrubbing the bath tub with cleanser to avoid a dirty ring—that it didn't do much good. Instead, I've started keeping lists of my accomplishments—little things that I've done day-to-day. Productivity is very important to me. If my results don't add up to what I think they should, my net worth in my own estimation goes down.

It's hard not to compare myself to others in this process. I have to fight feeling guilty that my house is not as neat as Ruth Ann's, my figure not like Georgia's, my patience not like Barbara's. Most of all, I feel guilty for letting Larry down. I suspect that others judge him, too, because I had a nervous breakdown. Do they think he has his priorities out of line? Spends too much time at the office or at church instead of home helping me? Will others still seek his counsel and advice?

So we talk about comparisons, Larry and I. Can we make horizontal comparisons instead of hierarchical ones? Can we avoid making impossible comparisons? We talk about it and that helps some. We list some of our accomplishments during the past month and discuss the choices we made to realize such achievements. For instance, one of mine is "I chose to take the kids to the park rather than clean the bathroom." This deliberate examination increases our awareness of what's happening in our lives. It also highlights that comparisons with others are impossible without knowing what choices someone else has made.

Joan, an old schoolmate, has recently become a frequent caller and visitor. When she calls, she always asks about Larry, the other children, and Steven. She doesn't respond much when I complain, but she does listen. In the last several months, she has developed a knack for "bumping into" people who have children with problems similar to Steven's. Or women who have been treated for depression. When she does not bring over a newspaper or magazine article on one of these topics, she sends them with a note, "Thought you'd be interested. Love, Joan."

Joan's support is a lifesaver to me. We are able to talk about some of my fears and problems and that helps relieve some of my stress. By seeing them clearly and giving them some "air time" with a friend, I find them much easier to deal with. I sometimes wish I could "start over," to recreate my past without a nervous breakdown. But I know that isn't possible. I can't simply dispose of my unwanted feelings in some leakproof, extra-heavy-duty trash bag, either. They are mine and I have to deal with them.

Some days, in quiet moments of reflection, I realize I have cut myself off from some who want to help and have justified my self-imposed isolation by noting to myself their clumsy attempts to reach me. I don't like admitting that at times I want to be offended and enjoy my self-pity. I hurt. I hurt the most for *me*. I want to be strong, to be seen as capable of doing some things very well. Maybe I can't do some things as well as I'd like and maybe I don't do other things well at all, but there are a few things I do very well. I have my lists of accomplishments as evidence.

I'm not certain that I've gotten over all of my "bad feelings" and depressive moments. There is still a lump in my throat when I think about various possibilities. I know I have not reached an emotional promised land since I still have both good and bad days. I really do love Steven very much, but his limitations sadden me. I want the best for him—just as I do for my other children—but I have learned to look for ways to see what is good for *him*, not just me. As I have given my fears their due instead of suppressing them, they have lost their stranglehold on me. I've been able to say, "So what?" Whenever I have worried about Steven's holding a job and taking care of himself when he grows older, it appears that lots of people don't seem to do that very well. I've put off deciding on his final earthly destiny. We'll have to work that out when it comes—just as with all my other children.

Once, in a family home evening, we talked about Steven's disability and my depression problem with our children, who then ranged in age from six to ten. We talked about the curiosity of other children when they notice

Steven's differences and our own reactions to them. We talked about acknowledging things we could not change, about accepting them while still setting goals and making plans for the future. We talked about the difference between acceptance and resignation. That family home evening was a turning point in my life. Instead of talking about what we *should* feel, we talked about what we *did* feel.

On that particular Monday evening, our oldest child was able to talk about how jealous she sometimes felt toward Steven. "You get excited when he does even ordinary things well, but you hardly notice me when I do something extra for you," she said to me. "Usually all I'll get is a 'thank you' and a tired kiss on the top of the head. I want to be noticed too." Since then, I have tried hard not to take our other children for granted, not to require great achievements just to get some ordinary praise.

Several weeks later a significant event occurred in our family which will forevermore be a beacon of faith and hope for me. One of the older boys came home from school and announced that he had made a new friend. "Can I invite him over for dinner?" he asked. "Sure," I replied. Then he said, "But, Mom, what about Steven?" My son recognized that he would have to do some explaining and answer some questions which would make him feel uncomfortable. I know because I had felt the same way many times myself. "What about Steven?" I asked. "Well, he's not like the other kids," he said. "No, he's not," I agreed, resisting my inclination to justify his disability. "He can't talk and does funny things sometimes," he continued. "That's right," I nodded, biting my lower lip to keep it from quivering. "Well, he's my little brother, and if John wants to come over and be my friend, he'll just have to understand."

I hugged my son before he went out to play. I think I've learned to understand, too.

5

Can I Ever Smile Again?

I sit alone sometimes in a darkened room. I like the feel of tranquility. Ordinarily, I am an active person who likes to be on the go. I like to go places, meet people, and do things. I have my civic projects and my church projects and also dabble in sales. I like to be involved. But quiet is also nice. It helps me to collect my thoughts and explore my feelings.

I try not to brood. I think I do very well, really. I am an optimistic person by nature and that helps me get through lots of the rough spots. The quiet helps, too. Maybe because it lets me sort through my feelings without interruption or truly think about God's majesty. Maybe because it lets me select which memories of Rebecca I will re-create in my mind and which remembrances I'll save for another time.

I loved Becky in the ways that all mothers love their children; delighting in her laugh, eager to teach her the wonders of the world, mindful to hold her just so in my arms every day and say, "I love you, little one." I miss those things. I miss them a lot. I've missed them ever since she was taken from me—stolen—without warning by someone I've never met and have never done any harm. Kidnapped. It happened to me, to my three-year-old Rebecca.

Such things cannot leave you unchanged. I am a different person than I was before this happened. Better in some ways, but not altogether better. I have not yet been able to note the passage of time by months. I divide my memories into two neat piles: before and after Rebecca. Since she has been gone less than a year, perhaps time itself will help remove this artificial clock.

Even now it is difficult sometimes to realize fully that it happened to me. My child, kidnapped. Everyone thinks that it will happen to someone else's children—or not at all. But it does happen. And it happened to me. I don't know why, but it did.

Jerry, my husband, and I have always tried to live the gospel and always expected Heavenly Father's protection in return. We paid our tithing, were married in the temple, had regular prayers, and accepted whatever church callings came to us. We had three wonderful children and were careful to teach them as well as we were able.

We tried to do our part to teach our children about the dangers of the world, too, and not simply rely on the Lord. For instance, I never let my children stray from me when we went out shopping together. When ten-year-old Melanie Larsen was abducted from her Layton, Utah, home, Jerry considered asking a friend to disguise himself and try to entice our children to go with him to emphasize the importance of not accepting favors from strangers. But he thought it was too scary to put the children through.

Nevertheless, our caution and training wasn't enough. Rebecca was stolen from us while playing with her brothers in a school playground which adjoins our backyard. She was taken against her will on that day which is now etched like a stone engraving in my memory. We never saw her again. Her lifeless body was found in a stream in Morgan Canyon about a month after her abduction, her feet bound together and her hands tied with a rope behind her back.

We had hoped and prayed for her safe return. We had printed handbills describing Rebecca and the man who took her from us and pleaded for her safe return on local and national television. We had a kidnap hotline put into our home. The police worked endlessly. The FBI came in from the very beginning. Fund raising went on in forms of donations and walkathons. Passport stops around the world were checked. We did not want to leave anything undone that we could do. Despite all our efforts, all our prayers, she was not safely returned to us. We had prayed as earnestly as we knew how, but our answer was not what we had hoped for.

Why not? Where were the promised blessings? Where were the miraculous events of protection I had heard so often in Sunday School as a student and repeated as a teacher? If anyone needed a blessing, we did. But it did not come as we had asked for it.

I felt angry. Betrayed. It was so unfair. So wrong. How could Heavenly Father allow such a cruel, unnecessary thing to happen? Accidents, illnesses, and problems happen. But to have a whole, healthy child stolen from your life is unthinkable. I bore her, nursed her, cared for her, and loved her dearly. For someone to take her from me was so wrong. So very wrong. How could this happen to me?

After the ordeal was over, I sat down on our sofa and cried. For a long time. Reality had ruined our hope. Our little daughter's life had flickered like a candle in the wind and then gone out. I felt so alone in the universe. I was an alien in my own neighborhood, unable to communicate or be understood. I resolved right then and there never to smile again or to laugh or to have a good time. The unspeakable had happened to me, and I was going to pay homage to Rebecca by deciding never to be cheerful again.

I became moody. Nothing pleased me. Everything was an irritation. I would burst out in tears at the slightest mention of Rebecca and sometimes sob uncontrollably for hours. I neither looked for nor allowed anyone to help. How could they? Had this happened to them? I felt like part of me was gone—empty, alone, out of place. Where could I go? Who could ever understand?

I went to Jerry and the Lord. Singly and together. After all, we had been through it together. They could understand. I didn't try to hide my feelings or control my emotions with them. And I didn't try to be strong for anyone. I talked to them—Heavenly Father and Jerry—about my anger and resentment and grief. I blamed them, then myself, then others. I wanted this tragedy to be taken back, to be given to someone else; it was a mistake that it had come to me anyway. I wanted to wake up and hold my Rebecca again and find out that it was all a bad dream. I wanted to turn the clock back and start all over again. But I couldn't. No matter how hard I tried to change the story, the ending was always the same. My little girl, my Rebecca, was gone!

Jerry let me talk. And so did Heavenly Father. They listened. And, eventually, so did I. I didn't like what I heard. I didn't like the person that I was becoming. But I owed it to Rebecca never to be happy again. I had made that pledge, hadn't I?

I continued this way for weeks, loathing myself and the world around me. I started to write my feelings in my journal—all of them. I didn't want to hold back anything. As I wrote, I was able to see my doubts, my fears. I wrote about my doubts concerning eternal life. Was it real? Other promises had not been provided to me as I had expected—promises of protection in exchange for righteous living—maybe this was a fraud, too? Who really knows for sure? I wanted to believe that Becky's spirit lived on in a glorious place in another world, but was it true? Or was it only what I wanted to believe?

I read everything I could. The scriptures. Books by LDS and non-LDS authors alike about the experience we call "death." I wanted to know where my Rebecca was. It became an obsession. While in this condition, I began resting on the couch one afternoon. As I lay there, I felt Rebecca come and lie on my chest. I stroked her hair and kissed her cheek and held her as tightly as I could. I would never let go of her again. When I came to myself, I was smiling with my arms folded on my chest. I got up and looked for her in the house, expecting her to be in another room. I called her name excitedly as I walked from room to room. No one answered. It was so real, so vivid. I knew she was there. I had held her in my arms; I knew I had. No longer do I doubt the reality of eternal life.

This opened a whole new horizon for me: God was listening after all. He was there. I wanted to know more. Why? Why me? Why anybody? Why not intervene in such circumstances and prevent them? Why not confuse such would-be assailants before they are able to harm innocent children? It would not have to be in a spectacular way. Do it quietly and without fanfare. Just do it. "Deliver us from evil," as Thou hast taught us to pray.

These questions rested oppressively on my mind like a heavy woolen blanket on a hot and humid summer night. They made me uncomfortable. Who was I to question God? I didn't like thinking them, but I wanted to know their answers. I wanted to know why things like this happened at all.

I told Jerry about these gnawing questions. And my father. Why can't I know? I deserve an explanation. We made a rule that when the three of us talked together that no thoughts were "unthinkable," no words were "unmentionable." If we were ever going to get over this tragedy and lift its oppressive weight from our lives, we must be able to say the worst, to get it out. There could be no value in being careful, in saying only the "right things." So we talked. We let our feelings take us wherever they would. We had no mapped-out route, no plans for arrival, no destination. These talks were wonderful. They let me see myself more clearly. Instead of denying my guilt and hurt and anger, I poured it out. Put it on the table in front of two people who I knew loved me very much. And I listened in return to their guilt and hurt and anger. When we legitimized our feelings, when we said it was okay to feel bad, we were able to see more objectively and in turn deal positively with those feelings. We set goals for ourselves regarding ways we were going to explore some negative feelings we had and how we were going to face up to them. Not grandiose goals. Little ones, in very ordinary circumstances. We wrote down as specifically as we could how we wanted to react when we felt lonely or started to blame ourselves or began thinking about the debilitating "what ifs"—"what if I had asked the children to help me in the house"; "what if I had gone to the store and taken them with me." We resolved together to consider no longer "what ifs." They were strictly off limits.

I had felt a confirmation from the Lord that I was a respected and loved daughter of His in a very personal way at a testimony meeting weeks before Becky was taken from me. I had felt His presence in a way that I had never experienced before or since, and I had felt a confirmation of my own self-worth. The Spirit bore witness to me that He lived. I do not know if He foresaw this tragedy and was preparing me for it or not. But I later recalled and clung to this experience as I explored my hurt and anger. I wanted again to feel those feelings. That gave me something to strive for, a place in my memory to return to and be refreshed. For if God lived, so did my Rebecca.

Knowing others cared for me and prayed for me sustained me tremendously in the three weeks between

Rebecca's abduction and the discovery of her little body. Such concern has not stopped in the months since then either. I've received letters from members of the Church from places as far away as Sri Lanka and as close as my next-door neighbor.

I do not believe this is something that had to happen. It was not a test designed for me or anyone else. It happened because someone abused his free agency. That person's gift from God took away my precious gift. Although there was no miraculous return of my Rebecca to me alive and unharmed, other miracles have occurred which have enabled me to go on living my life. The Lord has not left me comfortless.

I have broken my pledge to never smile or laugh again. I don't think I am "over" what happened to me and may never fully be in this life. I am changed forever. But my burden has been lifted, shouldered in part by others. Shouldered in part by my willingness to accept the reality of what happened to me—not as something which had to happen, just as something which did happen. There is no test intended only for me in what happened. In a horrible and unspeakable way, my child was taken from me. Despite my loss, I can recognize God found ways to quiet my fears and comfort my heart. Perhaps that is the greatest miracle of all. Instead of looking for His hand in events—either personal or global—I look inside my own heart. And when I sit by myself in a darkened room, I am not alone.

6

On My Own

After years of struggling through medical school and then residency, we were so pleased to be able to settle down at last. We went to Cedar City, Utah, where Kent, my husband was soon selected as chief of surgery at the small hospital there. A short time later he was called into the bishopric of our ward and I learned that I was pregnant with our fifth child. We were so glad that we had not waited until our schooling was finished and he was established in his profession to have a family. There had been some difficult years financially, but now that we were finally able to settle down, we didn't have to start from scratch in every aspect of our lives. We were young—I was barely twenty-eight—and had so much to look forward to together.

But all was not well in our Camelot. Kent began to experience some unaccounted-for dizziness at times. Then, a numbness around his mouth. At first the cause could not be determined. But after repeated tests in the following months, a specialist in Los Angeles detected what appeared to be a small tumor in his inner ear. Surgery was scheduled. It couldn't be delayed even though I was almost full term in my pregnancy. I didn't know if I could handle it very well emotionally, but we had no choice.

We knew the operation would not be easy. Kent put all of his office papers in order, anticipating a prolonged convalescence. Then we fasted and prayed. So did our ward. I was calm and tranquil, certain that this good man whom I loved dearly and who had so much to live for would be all right. He had prepared himself professionally to help others and alleviate suffering. He keenly felt this was a personal responsibility, almost as a calling from the Lord. Surely this operation would be but a short interlude as he now stood ready to use the years of training he had received. The doctors who operated on Kent emerged from the surgery with tight lips and drawn faces. The operation had been successful, but the tumor was much larger than anticipated. Kent was in critical condition. I went to his room in the intensive care unit and held his hand. He was not conscious, but I told him anyway all the reasons why he was going to recover. I reassured him.

Then, I found a private location at the hospital and locked the door to the room. I pleaded with the Lord, reminding Him of all the times I had secretly prayed to allow me eventually to die first, of the contentment that had come to me whenever I had such fears. I started to relax and felt a comforting arm on my shoulder. I felt as if my own father were present, holding me in his arms as he did when I was a child. I went back to Kent's side reassured. Everything would be all right after all. But Kent never regained consciousness and died early that next day.

I felt alone. Adrift. Like a ship severed from its moorings, left to float on the ocean without power and without a destination. Hadn't I felt reassured? Was it all simply my imagination? Was I set up? If this was some kind of test, it was bitter and cruel. Where am I going to go now for advice and help? With Kent gone, who am I going to rely on?

Ten days after Kent died, I gave birth to our fifth child. It was so unfair; he didn't even have a chance to see his own child. I was bitter. If the Lord needed someone to fill a statistical quota for tumors, why couldn't He have picked someone less deserving? Or, at least, someone older who had already lived a full life. We had only started. I just couldn't imagine life without him. For weeks afterward I was sure that every ache I had was a malignancy, every pain the beginning of a terminal malady. My own death was near at hand, I was certain, and so I made arrangements for the care of my children.

But I didn't die. Even though I sometimes wished I could. I missed him so much. Every time I read the scriptures, passages describing scenes where the prophets mourned because of the people's iniquity heightened my feelings of abandonment. I knew what Mormon meant when he wrote:

> And my soul was rent with anguish because of the slain of my people, and I cried,
>
> O ye fair ones, how could ye have departed from the ways of the Lord! O ye fair ones, how could ye have rejected that Jesus who stood with open arms to receive you.
>
> Behold, if ye had not done this, ye would not have fallen. But behold, ye are fallen, and I mourn your loss.
>
> O ye fair sons and daughters, ye fathers and mothers, ye husbands and wives, ye fair ones, how is it that ye could have fallen.
>
> But behold, ye are gone, and my sorrows cannot bring your return. (Mormon 6:16–19.)

Only I knew of nothing I had done to deserve my loss, no way to have prevented the occurrence.

After the casserole dishes and extra visits by sisters in

the ward waned, the reality of raising a family alone set in. The work and attention of a new baby helped divert my thoughts from brooding. It took so much energy to keep going in those first few months that I had little time left for anything else. I stayed by myself except for church attendance. I refused to go to ward socials or Single Adult-Special Interest Programs. I had known such a good marriage that I didn't want to be "available." I wanted to be by myself.

I think that was a mistake. I should have taken my time, to be sure. I should have waited until I wasn't feeling vulnerable but then gotten involved. It took me so long to get over my longing for the companionship of a man, someone to hold me tenderly and soothe my troubles. Because I tried to stay on the periphery of normal human relationships for so long, I was more susceptible to the attention of men I casually met. For almost two years, almost any man appealed to me. I didn't get out enough and mingle to overcome my vulnerability and loneliness. Paradoxically, I was scared of adjusting again to a marriage relationship and so stayed away from any single men my age. It probably didn't help that I was called to serve in the ward nursery, where I was even more isolated from other adults.

I tried to attend some medical meetings and to have dinner with other couples, but I felt so awkward that I stopped going to the former and ceased getting invitations to the latter. I didn't seem to fit in anywhere. Most of the friends I had were friends that Kent and I had together. Now that I was alone, those relationships were changed. Not because I or anyone else wanted them to, but simply because an essential element was missing. There was a missing ingredient in the recipe that had made us friends in the first place. Now, the mix was incomplete and could not be made up by what remained.

During my first year alone, I prayed with an intensity that I have not known since. I had no one else to turn to, so

I turned to the Lord. Such time on my knees was the only time I really felt good, included in something, part of an association beyond my own immediate family. Sometimes I would pray for more than an hour several times during the day, just because I didn't want the longing to return when I wasn't praying or doing necessary chores.

I may never have accepted Kent's death without a very important catalyst. I started attending the temple in St. George every other week. Not alone, but with eight others. All women. All widows. We talked about everything. There was no question that couldn't be asked. No topic that was taboo. Some were young, some middle-aged, and others elderly. Some were well-read and well-off, others were not. But we all shared something in common, besides a common heritage. We were experts in a particular aspect of life: being widowed. I have never looked forward to something so much in my life as these semi-monthly pilgrimages.

Although this group had no timetable for me to adjust and integrate back into ordinary living, they seemed to have an unspoken awareness of how I was doing. They wouldn't let me stand still. They wouldn't let me regress or give up. They had an intuitive sense of what it took to survive as well as progress and allowed only so much aimless wandering without some reality testing. I didn't know what they were doing to me until I looked back at how far I had come some time later. They gave me as many "resting places" as I needed, as long as I didn't try to set up camp along the way. They knew where they were going even if I didn't.

One of these friends urged me to write down all the things I would miss about Kent, to go beyond the trite phrases and predictable sentiments and be explicit about what I really liked about being with him. I put down not only the "highs" of shared experiences, but very ordinary events: tying the boat up when we went camping, crazy jingles he was always making up, the bacon and eggs he made on Sunday nights. Then I made a large scrapbook with my fondest memories of Kent in it. Somehow once this work was done and preserved, I was able to turn away from brooding on the past. It wasn't forgotten; I could turn back time by turning pages. Now, however, I was in control. I could decide when to relive them. Knowing they wouldn't be forgotten, I could go on.

After two years I decided to move, to start over somewhere else, to couple my emotional break with a geographical one. I walked through the empty rooms of our house in Cedar City before I let the memories of the good times Kent and I had together flood over me. I wasn't in a hurry. I relived some things, cried a little, even laughed out loud a little. I knew I wouldn't be coming back, and I wanted a complete benediction. I made some resolves, too. Not just about things I was going to do, but about the kind of mother and friend I was going to be. Compassionate. Independent. Practical. I could honestly say, "I don't have what I really want, but I am going to do the best I can with what I have."

I left looking straight ahead.

7

*I Can Never Again
Be What I Was*

I am a workaholic. It's true, I must confess. I've always been one. I was raised believing that I could do almost anything I wanted to do. I was taught that and I believed it. I still do.

I started out in the shipping industry as an office boy when I was seventeen years old. I worked part-time while going to college, then joined the military during World War II. After I got out, I got my old job back; after several years I was able to work myself up to Assistant Line Manager. My hard work was paying off. Then I had a great opportunity. My former boss left the company we worked for to start his own company. He needed experienced personnel. He wanted me.

I jumped at the chance. It was a small company, true. But it had a great future. It was an opportunity to start at the

ground floor of something and make it work. I had remained close to my old boss and respected him as an
executive and an individual. That was in 1963. There were
four people then. We worked hard, all of us. Fifteen- or
sixteen-hour days were not unusual. We had a dream, we
could see our potential, and we were willing to make it
work.

After a few years I moved to New York City to represent
our firm there. Our profit picture continued to improve and
our business continued to expand.

I moved back to our home office and was named vice-
president and general manager of the company. I was proud
of that, knowing that I had nurtured and shaped the company from its beginning. In seventeen years we had grown
from four to eighty employees. My job provided a comfortable living for my family, a challenge to me, and con-
tacts in the community to represent the Church. People
knew that I stood for high standards and hard work. I liked
being respected and able to represent my ideals to others
who would listen to what I had to say because of my
position.

All that changed almost overnight. In 1980, with interest
rates at an all-time high and a general economic recession,
one of the steamship companies we represented went bank-
rupt. Then another. And another. In three successive weeks
three major clients we represented closed their doors. We
were frantic. But we had faced tough challenges before and
would just have to generate some new business. We made
presentations everywhere trying to get some new clients.
But none were to be had. The story in our industry was the
same everywhere, even with our long-standing clients:
reorganizations, cutbacks, consolidations, and even
closings. There was no place to go, no other place to turn
to.

We struggled for months making staff reductions and
slashing expenses. But the handwriting was on the wall. We

had to sell. We had to merge with a bigger company while we still had some assets and our good name. We couldn't last. I put together a proposal and soon we had a buyer, a big outfit with a strong financial base and interest in the New Orleans market.

I stayed up all night sitting in my study staring at the walls after we sold the company. I felt as if I had given one of my sons or daughters to a stranger who visited my house —a stranger who promised to care for my child, but a stranger nonetheless. I was adrift at sea with no destination in mind.

The new company asked me to stay on, but in a much less responsible position. Still, it was a job. I wanted to work hard and show them that I could be a dedicated employee. I was as committed to the new company as I was to the one I had worked for so long. But things didn't work out for them. They were not familiar with operating in the New Orleans area and would not listen to me and others who wanted them to make a successful transition. And the economy, rather than improving, got worse. The recession deepened. After two years of trying to adapt, they gave up. They closed their local offices and laid off all of their New Orleans employees. Me included.

I was bewildered. Where would I go? What would I do? I was forty-five years old; I couldn't start over again. I brooded. I didn't want to do anything. I was embarrassed. How could I face people? How could I continue in the bishopric, continue to counsel others about their personal lives when mine was in such a shambles? I didn't even have a job! I felt so overwhelmingly incompetent.

After several weeks I was finally able to bring myself to put together a resume. I read the jobs section of the newspaper and visited several recruiting firms. I wrote old friends and former associates. I hated doing that most of all. I felt that I was using them, using our friendship in an inappropriate way.

Unemployed. I was unemployed. Suddenly, I felt uncomfortable in social situations. New members of the ward would ask what I did and I would have to repeat the word again. I tried saying it differently: making a career change, looking for new opportunities, moving between jobs. Regardless of what words I said, it still sounded like "unemployed" to me. And I felt ashamed every time I had to say it.

We had some savings, but as the weeks stretched into months without a job that was soon gone. I thought about just taking a job, any job—gas-station attendant, security guard, janitor—but was strongly advised by a job-placement counselor not to do so. He said I would be stuck in that line of work. I didn't know how I could ever be more stuck than I was. So my wife and I talked it over and decided to sell our car and buy a cheap model—and for her to go to work.

I could take living on a restricted income. I could take the belittling that went with standing in unemployment lines. I could take the loss of status and esteem. I couldn't take Marge working when I wasn't. I couldn't take it. I *had* to get a job. No matter what. I was at rock bottom.

I needed help. I prayed for something to change. I think I know how a farmer prays who is desperate for rain for his crops. I was just as desperate. I tried to keep busy. I had always spent a lot of time in my calling in the bishopric, but I doubled my efforts. I didn't want to leave anything undone. I wanted my life to be as pure as possible. I wanted to merit any blessings that proper living could qualify for. I didn't want to leave anything to chance. Still, nothing happened.

Lots of people I knew tried to encourage me. They told me something would turn up. They told me not to worry about it. Easy for them to say.

Yet I knew they were sincere. They wanted to help. They made suggestions and asked about leads. But when I had a couple of interviews and didn't get the job, it was tough to have others ask me how it went. I didn't want to admit to myself that I didn't get the job, let alone to anyone else.

I'm not the kind of guy who likes to talk about my problems to others. I suppose that's not very good. I really don't know. But it's me. What helped me during this period was playing golf with Gene and Ken every other Saturday, as we had for years. They acted like nothing changed. They didn't try to pay for things or ask me questions. They just played golf. It gave me stability. Outside the Church, it seemed like the only thing that wasn't going topsy-turvy. I looked forward to them. They were my oasis, my chance to get away from it all. Although I sometimes brought up being out of work, neither Gene nor Ken ever mentioned it. They let me say what I wanted to and that was it. I felt as if I were writing my frustrations on a blackboard that would be erased when I finished. I didn't have to justify or explain anything. It was wonderful.

After eight months I finally got another job. I am literally making one-third the income I was making previously. My life-style has changed dramatically and—in all likelihood—changed permanently. I'm a small cog in a big wheel. I've lost something, a sense of place, that I doubt I'll ever recover. I think I know what Southerners felt like after the Civil War—a loss that I'll feel forever.

I've tried not to become embittered by my new situation. It hasn't always been easy. I realize bad things happen and that one of life's misfortunes has happened to me. I wish I could have been smarter and found a job just as good as the one I had. I wish that things had turned out another way. But they just didn't. This has happened to me. It didn't have to happen. I don't think there's a plan that says it had to happen; it just happened. I'm convinced that some bad things happen to all of us. The challenge of life is not to become embittered or cynical about them but to do our best regardless of what happens. After all, we are really not in any kind of race to see or do or accumulate so much stuff. We are simply going through a process of growth that has unanticipated turns and unforeseen detours. When I remind myself of such facts, I am not discouraged.

8

Two Is Even, One Is Odd

As a young girl in Primary, and later as a teenager in YWMIA, I can recall several lessons on the importance of a temple marriage. I think it was emphasized as much to the girls as going on a mission was to the boys. I remember the care which Sister Hutchinson, in particular, would take to prepare us for our callings as wives and mothers. She was a kindly woman who helped us embroider samplers of the Salt Lake Temple, memorize the words of Ruth to Naomi, and tell us stories about her early courtship and marriage. I thought then, and believe just as firmly now, that "marrying the right person at the right time and in the right place" is a vital goal for every woman.

Some people are shocked to discover this when they first meet me. They assume that because I am an unmarried medical doctor that I have chosen a professional life-style in

lieu of raising a family. They expect me to be pushy and demanding and to defend "women's rights" in every conversation. Even some whom I associate with regularly question
my sincerity regarding gospel truths. I think they expect a
single professional woman to fit a certain stereotype and do
not know how to deal with someone who doesn't.

I have never paid much attention to what other people
thought. I grew up in a small town in rural Idaho and didn't
care that I was called a "tomboy." I've always liked animals
and am almost as interested in training quarter horses as I
am in treating newborn children. During my undergraduate
work at Brigham Young University, I considered the religion
classes as stimulating as the science courses. I've always
found a commitment to both very easy.

I never thought much about getting married or becoming
a doctor when I was receiving my medical training. I
accepted both as ordinary goals which I would surely realize
with time. Now that I've obtained one, I'm not at all certain
about the other.

I think my uneasiness about ever marrying has gone
through a distinct cycle, and only now do I find it possible
to talk about it objectively. In my mid-twenties, my attitude
was "silently hopeful." I realized after graduating from
Brigham Young University that statistically my chances of
marrying were substantially reduced. But I also reasoned
that I wasn't looking for a lot of suitors—one would do. As
the years progressed, I saw that my chances were diminish-
ing. In my late twenties I became despondent. I had a lot of
agonizing moments during this period. I questioned
whether I had sold my "birthright"—my goal of celestial
marriage—for a mess of pottage. I questioned my motiva-
tion for pursuing a medical degree and my place in the
order of things. I didn't seem to fit in anywhere. The other
women medical students saw me as prudish and afflicted by
my heritage. The sisters at Relief Society were simply inter-

ested in other things—mainly their husbands and children. I didn't relate to anyone.

I met a man during this period whom I cared for a great deal. He was good and capable and honest, but not a member of the Church. And he didn't have the same standards that I had. I was uncertain that I had always traveled the right road before, but I *was* certain that there were some things that would not be compromised in my life. Reserving normal marital relations for marriage was among them. I simply was not going to place myself in the kind of circumstances where I would be vulnerable.

He didn't understand. We dated for several years. We shared our goals, our hopes, our wishes. I had a serious surgical operation—a rare and dangerous pituitary tumor was creating chemical imbalances in my body—and he was with me before the procedure and during my convalescence. He had interrupted his schedule and work routine to go to this out-of-state hospital. All these things we shared together.

And then he left. He couldn't accept the Church and its teachings, and I couldn't imagine life any other way. He found someone more accommodating.

Some friends have told me about the loneliness they have felt in their marriages: a husband who is absorbed in his work, in getting ahead and being a success, with little time or energy left over for anything else. Or one who is consumed by sports and plays on every ward and city ball team, spending the remainder only with their boys helping them develop their athletic skills. I sense the loneliness that especially a woman feels when the light has gone out between her and her husband. I don't think it compares to the loneliness I felt at that time in my life. I had no anchors, no one who depended on me. It is an awful feeling not to be needed.

I wonder if those who are married realize how much they take dependency on one another for granted. Even in bad marriages, there is a kind of security that comes from being able to rely on someone else for certain things and knowing in return that others depend on you. I suppose that's why some battered wives would rather stay married than go out on their own.

I struggled with my values and with my own sense of self-worth. I had always believed in a gospel of hope and had reveled in this Book of Mormon passage: "Wherefore, whoso believeth in God might with surety hope for a better world, yea, even a place at the right hand of God, which hope cometh of faith, maketh an anchor to the souls of men, which would make them sure and steadfast, always abounding in good works, being led to glorify God" (Ether 12:4).

I felt like the father of the afflicted child, who came to the Savior seeking a blessing. When questioned concerning his faith, he "said with tears, Lord, I believe; help thou mine unbelief" (Mark 9:24).

I felt the pressure of several "double binds" that I knew I had to resolve if I were ever to climb out of the abyss of despondence I was in. I had been taught as a young woman to be feminine and demure and a little passive, but also to develop my talents aggressively and be prepared to serve others. I had sensed the need for career interests—to rely on if I was not to have the emotional lifeline of marriage. But I was warned that becoming a doctor could be very intimidating to potential suitors. I could not reconcile being competent and appearing frail.

I started attending Single Adult firesides and conferences and found some helpful. Some of the speakers approached their topics in a very patronizing and condescending way, telling those present that the Lord loved them and not to worry about their single status. Their well-meaning advice to the women, in particular, to lose weight, dress stylishly, be more positive and try harder sent an unfortunate message to many: "You're not okay—if you had only done

things differently, this would not have happened to you."
The regular reiteration "I know how you feel" only
communicated that they really didn't want to be bothered
with anyone else's problems. But others spoke about their
losses, their disappointments, their aspirations and found
receptive minds and hearts. I remember a sensitive discus-
sion by a high councilor who told of his frustrations at
being barely able to read and his efforts at self-teaching, and
another from a bishop with a wayward son. They showed
me themselves; and I saw how others accepted that something was missing from their lives, something they wanted
very badly, but did not have.

I remember sitting down after one fireside determined to
write a profile of who I was and of the kind of person I
wanted to be. I listed what I liked about myself, my values,
my interests, my hang-ups, my fears, what I did well, things
I always wanted to do, things I never wanted to do. I wanted
to leave some of the "old me" behind and go on to other
things. I wanted to stop feeling sorry for myself because of
the things I didn't have. I wanted to—for me. So . . . I cut
my hair, started a photo album of favorite places, traded in
my old bike for a new one, and went to Europe. I am a
planner, a careful person by nature, and I just did some im-
pulsive things, things I had really wanted to do. It was wonderful. Changing some things outwardly helped me make
some inward changes. I felt like a new person.

I am more prepared for living now than I have been in
years. People say that it goes with being in my thirties. But
I'm not sure that age has as much to do with it as coming to
terms with myself. That's not to say I cope well every day.
Sometimes I get so physically exhausted from the hospital
routine, from seeing so much pain and suffering, that I want
to fall apart. At times I'll deal with it by sleeping fourteen to
sixteen hours in a row or bicycling up Emigration Canyon
until my legs are numb. Both are good stress-reduction
methods for me. Then sometimes I'll indulge in escape—go

to three movies in an afternoon or eat a large pizza all by myself. Some days it's better not to fight it; it'll pass.

There is something that's good and right and honorable that's missing in my life. I know that. If I never marry, I will be sad for what I miss. There is a place in me, a little corner that is empty. I would like it occupied, but not at any cost. There are some things which are too dear to trade away just to fill that void. I can give those feelings their due and go on. I can stop trying either to deny those feelings or to try to make up for them. They have their small place, but no more. There are other things which I do have, and they are very good, too. When I find the possibilities within myself, they seem to crowd out what I don't have. My capabilities, my sense of self-worth, my spiritual confirmation that the Lord loves me and is pleased with me become enough for now.

And now is all I know. I have stopped wishing for a different tomorrow and accepted today for what it is. If it is not everything I want, it is at least some of the things I want. There are "downs" but there are also "ups." I am not a Pollyanna; I've seen too much pain and suffering in my profession to accept carelessly every event as "for the best" (as some who practice the power of positive thinking might suggest). But there are many good and precious things in my life, and I'm not going to lose them by either ignoring them or wishing I have something I don't have. I have disappointments, but also some satisfactions which are very deep and personal and real. They are mine. They cannot be taken from me. And I will not give them up voluntarily.

9

Looking Forward to Tomorrow

Darkness began to loosen around the palm trees that are so characteristic of southern California as another new day began. I got up, dressed, fixed breakfast, and sent David off to work and the kids off to school just as I had so many other days. I liked the calm which followed my family's departure. It gave me time to sit down with two-year-old Jamie and to play without any other distractions. "They grow up so fast, change so much at this age," I thought to myself. I didn't want to be a bystander in my children's growth; I wanted to be a participant.

That evening when everyone came home, I had dinner all prepared. I had Primary inservice meeting to attend and wanted to have it as easy for David as possible. The other kids were playing in the backyard when I was ready to leave. I kissed David good-bye and told him to keep an eye on everyone, especially Jamie.

"He's been getting into everything lately. And he likes to hide in things to tease me," I reminded David.

"Well, I just saw them all playing on the jungle gym, so they'll be easy to take care of until it's time to come in for their baths," he said.

I walked out the front door and behind the car to open the gate that spanned our driveway, then back around the car again before sliding into the driver's seat. Many children in our neighborhood often left things in our driveway, and I had a habit of walking around the car to make certain there weren't any toys left there. I started the car and backed out of our angled driveway. I hit something. Whatever it was must have been hidden under the car. I got out to see what it was. "Oh, no!" I screamed. It was Jamie.

I dropped to my knees, holding my head with my hands and yelling for David. In an instant David was out the front door. I don't remember much of what happened next. The trip to the hospital, David blessing Jamie, the doctors' methodical efforts to save Jamie's life, the awful stillness in the waiting room. Despite our prayers, despite the prayers of our bishopric and my visiting teachers who waited for us, Jamie's spirit left his body that night. We could not make him stay.

The only time I could ever remember going to a hospital was to have a baby. I felt so awkward going home empty-handed. I felt so alone in the universe. Abandoned. Left to myself in a foreign land with a language I did not understand and people I did not recognize. I don't remember much of the weeks that followed, either. I cried inconsolably for days, would not get out of bed, did not want to talk to anyone, would hold David at night afraid to go to sleep.

After several weeks David and I sat down together and talked about our lives. What were we going to do? How were we going to handle Jamie's death? How were we going to regard each other? Someone had given us an article on how parents cope with the accidental death of a child. The article reported that nearly 90 percent of such families break apart. They do not cope. We resolved during that evening together to take one day at a time. We needed each other. We relied on each other. Somehow, we would go on together. We made a solemn and sacred vow to one another: we would not blame each other for what happened. We each had enough of a burden, we would not add to the load by hardening our hearts towards one another.

But this resolve did not relieve my own self-loathing. How could I have done such a horrible thing? I was haunted by "should haves" and "what ifs." I should have checked underneath the car . . . I should have looked in the backyard . . . what if I had not accepted my Primary calling? . . . what if I had called someone to give me a ride? I was beside myself. I didn't know where to turn. I wanted to find a place to hide, to stay there forever. But there was no place to run to.

A friend from college came and stayed with us for several weeks. She was so good to me and for me. We reminisced, and it helped to be reminded of good times. Near the end of her stay she sat down with me on the couch and put her two hands on my shoulders and literally shook me. "Becky," she said, "you've got to stop feeling sorry for yourself. You have four beautiful children and a husband who loves you dearly. It's time to put the past behind you."

I know she meant well, but I didn't want to put the past behind me. I couldn't. I didn't deserve to. I needed to do penance. But for what? What had I done wrong? What sin had I been guilty of? What did I need to repent of? Carelessness, was that it? But who looks underneath a car? Who was more careful than I in the many ordinary, everyday endeavors of running a household?

David and I decided to get away for the weekend together. We needed time to think. Time to plan. We rented a cabin in the mountains and just spent time together. That Sunday we attended church in a rustic building that swelled with weekenders and vacationers. The Relief Society room was filled to capacity. It was the spiritual living lesson. The teacher was well-prepared and began discussing the blessings that we can expect through righteous living. Then she told what I am certain she intended to be a faith-promoting story to illustrate the concept she was teaching. Her family was camping. They had a large recreational vehicle they were backing into a designated parking space. Their ten-year-old son was giving directions. He tripped on a fallen tree limb. His father didn't see the fall. He backed over his son. The boy's leg was broken but he was otherwise unhurt. Miraculously, he healed with no complications. The teacher bore testimony that such protection was our right and privilege if we lived righteously.

I had to leave. I couldn't stay. What had I done wrong? Even if I had done something wrong, surely Jamie should not be responsible for my actions. Where was a miracle when I needed one? I knew this teacher's testimony was true, but I had also searched my heart and sensed that the promise of righteousness was not an exemption from difficulties. It was not consolation for me, either, to acknowledge that Jamie was destined for celestial glory and was no doubt with family members on the other side of the veil. I wanted to hold my little one now. I didn't want to wait.

Six weeks after the accident I began attending church in our home ward again. We arrived early and sat near the back. As other families began filling the chapel, I couldn't help but notice the two-year-old boys. One began playing with a blanket, teasing his mother just the same way Jamie had teased me. I went to pieces. I sobbed uncontrollably and went to the foyer. From then on, we always sat on the front row.

There were so many good friends at church who wanted to help me, to comfort me, to extend a helping hand. I could see it in their eyes, and that did help. But most of them felt so uncomfortable, shifting from foot to foot when our eyes would meet and hurrying on after greeting me. I felt so alone, trying to keep my family going and putting the pieces back together in my own life. I needed someone to turn to, someone outside the family to talk to who could understand what I was going through and help me pull through it. I felt I was going under—drowning—in sight of help, but no one noticed me.

Then Earlene came. She knocked on my door unannounced. She was from another ward in our stake. Someone had offhandedly mentioned our accident to her. She had found out where we lived and started to call one day last week, but put the phone down before it started to ring. She didn't want to intrude. But she didn't feel right. Restless. Dissatisfied. She didn't know why. Finally, she put on her make-up, curled her hair, put on her favorite dress, and came to my house. She sat in the car for nearly forty-five minutes. She almost hadn't come in.

She told me she had been living in Utah and was doing the wash while her children were playing in the back. Somehow her three-year-old got through the gate and wandered into the front yard. He fell into an irrigation ditch, and two agonizing days later his body was recovered six miles from home. It was four years ago. It still hurt to talk about it.

I broke down and sobbed. We cried together. And we prayed together. She left two hours later. She was just what I needed but didn't know what to look for, let alone whom to ask. She was a confirmation that the Lord loved me and heard my prayers.

Earlene introduced me to a self-help group that a local hospital was sponsoring for parents who had lost children. She knew the nurse who was sponsoring it and knew of her religious convictions, even though she was not LDS. I attended hesitantly at first, but after attending monthly for several months, I was able to fully participate—even to talk. I saw that my anger and bitterness and resentment were normal. Earlene would come over after these meetings, too, and we would talk. I don't know why I needed her to tell me, "It's okay to cry, to feel bad," but I did. I needed someone outside my family—someone I didn't have to be strong for—to legitimize it for me.

Knowing that Earlene had survived, had gone on, gave me tremendous hope. Sometimes we read the scriptures together and talked about their meaning for us. I am particularly grateful for a pronouncement of Paul's in the New Testament:

> Therefore being justified by faith, we have peace with God through our Lord Jesus Christ:
>
> By whom also we have access by faith into this grace wherein we stand, and rejoice in hope of the glory of God.
>
> And not only so, but we glory in tribulations also: knowing that tribulation worketh patience;
>
> And patience, experience; and experience, hope. (Romans 5:1–4.)

As I began to recover my self-worth, I regained hope. Hope not only in an eternal future, but also hope for me in an ordinary present. I craved to once again consider myself just an ordinary person with ordinary reactions to everyday events. I started calling my visiting teachers just to see what they were doing. I would ask them what they had done the day before and they agreed to report on mundane activities: feeding a small child, preparing a family home evening lesson, attending a PTA meeting. I found myself vicariously sharing their ordinary joys and concerns and relearning how it felt to have them.

Our home teachers helped, too. Shortly after the accident, Brother Matthews came to our door. He is a plumber and an excellent handyman who had helped David fix several things in the six months he and his fourteen-year-old son had been our home teachers. He is a quiet man who has difficulty giving a prepared lesson and would usually have his son leave a message based on the First Presidency message in the *Ensign*. He stood at the door with his hands thrust deeper in his pockets than I thought possible. He asked David to collect all of the shoes in the house and sent his son to accompany my husband in picking them all up and putting them in a tattered sack. Later that evening his son returned them, each pair conspicuously polished. He never spoke to us directly about the accident, but in this and lots of other little ways he conveyed that his thoughts were with us and he was pulling for us.

It has been two years since Jamie died. Two long years. Two painful years. I have learned much. I have made peace with myself. I am surviving. I would have never thought that possible two years ago. I owe a great debt to my Father in Heaven for the peace He has spoken to my heart. For Earlene, whom He would not let stay home. For Brother Matthews and for others. I have learned so much about compassion through Jamie's death. I would trade it all to still have him with me, but I cannot. I cannot go back, so I am going forward. Halting, stumbling, perhaps, but going forward nonetheless.

I am changed forever. I know that now and have accepted it. Not in a melancholy way. I am past that. I don't know how to describe it exactly. It's not that I'm "over" the accident. I don't think I ever will be, even though I no longer flinch when I hear an ambulance's siren. There is a part of me that will always long for Jamie. But now it is a little corner in my life. It has its place, but its bounds are fixed. It has its limits. It cannot pass. It is one event in my life—an important one to be sure—but there are many important others, too. It is one among many.

It took some time to realize that. But not just the passage of time. There is some truth to the old saying that time heals all wounds. But it is not time alone that heals. Time helps in gaining a perspective on such events, but I am convinced that we must come to terms with them by willingly voicing our worst fears. We must reach inside ourselves and lay bare our very souls—to ourselves. The process is often painful, but necessary. Unless we acknowledge our bitterness and doubts, we will not work through them but will likely become cynical and resentful. The scriptures record this important dialogue between the Savior and a troubled father: "Jesus said unto him, If thou canst believe, all things are possible to him that believeth. And straightway the father of the child cried out, and said with tears, Lord, I believe; help thou mine unbelief." (Mark 9:23–24.)

God can heal broken hearts. He can help unbelief. He can restore life. He restored mine. I poured out all my bitterness and envy and resentment over the loss of my son. And when it was all spilled and none was left and I was empty and alone, I began my life again.

10

Too Much Caring to Give Up

I like to pause for a moment as I look into the faces of the congregation when I conduct a sacrament or priesthood meeting. I like the feeling at such times that comes of being part of a grand and glorious movement that is bigger than life itself. Sometimes I stand at the podium too choked up to speak, awed that God would include even me in this plan. I don't mean to be overly sentimental, it's just that such feelings are sometimes overwhelming.

Life has been so good to Julie and me. We have been blessed with four healthy sons. I've progressed in my career, relocating occasionally to accept positions of increasing responsibility. We like Dallas, our new home, where even Matt, our second son, who sometimes had difficulty making friends, seemed to be fitting in.

That's what bothered me; Matt's friends. He'd become well acquainted with a boy in the ward who was a member of the Church in name only. I didn't think he was a very good influence on Matt, who was more vulnerable to the influence of others than any of his brothers. In fact, in the last few months I had noticed some subtle changes in Matt —his clothes, his speech, his habits—that were not very positive, so I decided to talk to him about it. Without being overbearing, I wanted to remind him of the standards in our family and encourage him to seek out some other friends who shared values more like his own.

When we first talked, I was stunned by his reply. He accused me of hypocrisy. Brent, his older brother, was on a mission bearing testimony to others, he said, while he was trying to do the same at home. Why was it okay for Brent to associate with others with different values and not okay for him? He reminded me that I had discussed the need for fellowshipping those who were inactive by being tolerant and nonjudgmental at sacrament meeting three weeks ago. Were those insincere remarks, appropriate for the occasion but with no real meaning, he questioned.

I responded clumsily. I wasn't sure what to say. Although I told him that I was interested in his welfare and concerned about the negative influence of his newfound friends, my words didn't have a positive impact. In fact, during our conversation things got worse instead of better. Matt said that I didn't understand him, that I didn't trust him or I wouldn't worry about others having a negative influence on him. He said that if I really trusted him, I wouldn't treat him like a baby and try to protect him from worldly influences. He asked me to believe in him and give him a chance to prove that he could be a positive influence on others.

I loved Matt, I wanted him to believe in himself; I wanted his fragile self-confidence to be boosted, and so I gave him a hug and my consent. But also a condition: if he was going to be a missionary, he needed a plan and someone with whom to discuss his progress. I volunteered for the job. Matt was disturbed by this turn of events, but despite believing it was unnecessary, he reluctantly agreed to it. We set up a schedule to discuss activities and plans weekly.

It was more difficult than I thought it would be to actually have such sessions. In the ensuing weeks, it seemed my travel schedule for my business was unusually heavy. Matt, too, was often unavailable for interviews we had arranged in advance. When we did meet, his plans for actual fellowshipping were vague. He resisted most of my suggestions as too old-fashioned or irrelevant. He wanted to do things his own way, he said.

Matt often came home from a party or high school activity with alcohol- and tobacco-smelling clothes. He admitted that some of his friends drank beer and smoked cigarettes, but he insisted that he never did. He said that his example was having a positive impact on his friends and some had even inquired about attending church with him. He reminded me that Jesus had been accused of being a sinner because he associated with people who were not acceptable to the Jewish ruling classes. Matt encouraged me to continue to trust him.

I had an uneasy feeling about Matt's ready answers during such discussions. He always seemed to know exactly what to say as if he were simply repeating rehearsed remarks. In my personal prayers, my uneasiness returned when I talked to the Lord about Matt. Something was not right about the tales he was telling me, but I had nothing except my internal discomfort to go on. When I confronted Matt with these impressions, he defiantly maintained that he was not involved in anything wrong and that I should not worry so much about him.

It was the phone call from school that signalled things had gotten out of hand. Matt had been truant for the second time and would now be suspended for three days. "The

second time? When was the first time?'' my wife questioned
the caller. The school secretary excused herself for a
moment and retrieved a note from her files. My wife's signature was on the note dated several weeks ago, the secretary
said.

It was difficult to control my anger when I confronted
Matt that night. I had trusted him, I told him, and he had
violated that trust. He had missed school, forged his
mother's signature, and doubtless lied to us about other
things. Matt tried to pacify me. It wasn't as bad as it
seemed, he said. He had made a mistake in going off with
someone else and had gotten caught, that was all. I ex-
ploded. "That was all? That was all? Isn't that enough?''

Matt got up and started to leave the room, saying that he
wasn't in the mood to be yelled at. I shoved him back in his
seat, telling him I didn't care what kind of mood he was in—
we needed to get some things straightened out right then
and there. He sprang to his feet and pushed me—harder
than I was prepared for—almost knocking me to the floor. I
doubled up my fist and headed back for him.

I don't know what I might have done if Julie had not
stepped between us. She calmed both of us down, redi-
rected our anger, and suggested we work things out tomorrow when we were both calmer.

I didn't sleep well that night. It wasn't just Julie's muffled
sobbing into the pillow, or the haunting question of
whether I would have actually struck my own son. What
bothered me most was that I was uncertain what I should do
next. "What are we going to do? What are we going to do?''
Julie had asked me over and over that night. I didn't have an
answer. I felt like a swimmer caught in a strong undertow
being pulled under water. I was drowning and couldn't even
make out the shore. I simply didn't know what to do.

In the weeks that followed, I talked to my closest friends
and relatives about Matt, including my own father in Salt
Lake City. Some of these friends and relatives also talked

and listened to Matt and encouraged him as much as they could. None of it seemed to work. We came home from a youth activity that Matt had not been allowed to attend, to the smell of marijuana in his room. There was also a marijuana pipe under his bed, which he claimed a friend had left there.

It didn't stop there either. Loose change and other unattended money left around the house began disappearing. Not long after his three-day suspension, Matt was permanently ejected from school for truancy. With each new incident, an angry confrontation occurred at home, resulting in more restrictions imposed on his activities.

Matt's behavior was tearing our family apart. His two younger brothers pleaded in their prayers for him to "get better" and become part of the family again. They avoided participating in church activities, vaguely feeling out of place. Julie and I had harsh words with each other as we argued over being too hard or too soft on Matt.

When Matt finally returned from an unplanned and unexplained two-day absence over Memorial Day, something had to be done. I told him that he was no longer welcome in our house. His actions were completely unacceptable and would not be tolerated. If he was unwilling to abide by the most basic rules of our household, he would have to live elsewhere—because of my love for him as my son. I said that I would make arrangements for him to stay with a relative and would require that certain rules be obeyed. Saying these words was the hardest thing I've ever done in my life.

Matt was shocked. Perhaps because he expected anger and shouting, he was taken back by my calm resolve. He said that he didn't know what to do. He needed time to think. Softly, I told Matt how much I truly loved him and that he could take the time he needed. I indicated that I thought he needed to get out of the environment he had created and start fresh somewhere else. Then he could return and be welcomed home with open arms.

Matt didn't give us an answer for several weeks. He obeyed family rules, but kept himself apart from any interaction with us. He was more like a boarder than a family member. I worried if I had merely obtained outward compliance at the cost of never again having Matt feel loved and accepted by me.

Early one afternoon, I received a phone call at the office. It was Matt. Could I meet him? I cancelled several meetings and picked him up at home. We drove around town in silence for quite awhile before stopping at a hamburger stand. It was there that he broke down, sobbing uncontrollably. He couldn't handle his life, he said. There were too many pressures. He was using drugs and had been involved in taking joy rides in other's cars. He wanted to accept my offer to go stay with a relative.

Within three days, Matt was on an airplane to Salt Lake City. He attended summer classes at a high school there while living with his grandparents to make up lost time due to his suspension from school in Dallas. Despite some lingering defiance and resentment, he seemed to be making progress as the summer days passed. Being somewhere else with similar household rules and a supportive environment were having a positive effect.

When the phone rang late one Saturday evening, a lump came to my throat. Something was wrong with Matt. I could sense it. When I answered the phone, I found out that my senses were right. But it was a different problem than I had guessed. Matt had been in an automobile accident and was in intensive care at a local hospital.

Matt's leg was severely mangled and for ten days there would be some question about whether it should be amputated. If his leg could be saved, the doctors said that he would never walk again without great effort.

Rather than welcoming us when we arrived at the hospital, Matt treated us with anger and resentment. "What are you doing here?" he growled. "I bet you think this is just what I deserved." Rather than giving him the reply he expected, Julie tenderly teased him. "You know how we enjoy antagonizing you, Matt. Now that you're strapped into a hospital bed, you can't get away from us by going to your room." As she so often did, Julie knew just the right thing to say to disarm him.

Matt stayed in the hospital for twenty-eight days. Julie or I stayed with him during every one of them. Months of wearing braces, walking on crutches, and undergoing physical therapy followed. In retrospect, it was perhaps the best thing that could have happened to Matt. We talked and laughed and played games together during that recuperation period that would never have been possible if he had not been injured. More importantly, he had an obstacle to overcome now, a difficulty to conquer. He had something to work for. For the first time in his life, he had a goal that was important to *him*.

Matt's struggle to overcome his physical handicap gave him a sense of control over his own world that he had never felt before. Despite intense pain, he exercised religiously. He saw that his own efforts made a difference in what happened to him. Perhaps his victories were not grandiose, but they belonged to him. And he was winning.

Matt's newfound self-confidence affected him in other ways, too. He started studying in school, determined to make up for lost time. For the first time ever, he began to read the scriptures and ask me questions about them. Seeing that he could overcome an external adversity transformed him. It was also a visible symbol of an inner journey he had undertaken. He began to set and achieve other self-directed goals.

Matt's talking about serving a mission now. Since he's twenty he can go virtually anytime he's ready. That's the point, he says, he wants to be ready before he's called. He wants to serve for the right reasons. Two years ago he said that he didn't want to serve a mission because he didn't want to be a "carbon copy" of Brent. He wanted to be his own person and not live in Brent's shadow. Now, he thinks a mission may be right for *him*.

I feel uncomfortable when people say that Matt's "turned out" all right after all. I don't think raising children is equivalent to a manufacturing process, so I don't believe that we've ever "got it made." Parents are not two people waiting for their children to grow up and leave, but are instead affected greatly by their children's influence on them. I still wince each time I see a child, no matter at what age, disobey his parents. Some things leave us changed forever.

I have always wanted the best for Matt, that hasn't changed. But something about that desire has changed. I want the best for *his* sake, not mine. I was embarrassed and ashamed at Matt's rebellious behavior as a teenager. I often wondered at such times if I shouldn't be released from my church calling. How could I expect to help lead the ward when I couldn't effectively lead my own household? Now, I see such a perspective is presumptuous at best. We don't lead anyone, we only help them find themselves.

I've framed a statement made by Elder Marvin J. Ashton and hung it in my office as a reminder that when you care enough, you never give up.

"I believe we start to fail in the home when we give up on each other. We have not failed until we quit trying. As long as we are working diligently with love, patience, and long-suffering, despite the odds or the apparent lack of progress, we are not classified as failures in the home. We only start to fail when we give up on a son, daughter, mother, or father."

This statement has a unique meaning for me.

11

In the Gospel Net

I looked at those sixteen solemn faces. Some old, some young. Some with somber eyes, some glazed with tears. It was not easy to tell the stake presidency and high council that I had committed an infidelity. It was humiliating beyond expression. These were men I knew and respected and sensed they had respected me in return. But, there was no denying it, I had broken a sacred promise made in the most sacred place on earth. I had violated the trust extended to me by the Lord and by the members of my ward. I had to be excommunicated. And that day I was. I was no longer worthy to be called a Latter-day Saint.

I left that high council court with remorse, but no bitterness. I had a testimony of the gospel of Jesus Christ; I knew it was true. What was done had to be done. There was no other way.

I had asked my wife to remain at home even though she wanted to go with me, wanted to wait in the church foyer for me. I wanted to go alone. And alone I was. I drove to a nearby park and sat on a park bench. It was winter and was snowing. No one else was there. The snow swirled, making it difficult to see. I was lost, I thought to myself. I had failed. I had gained a measure of respect in my life only to have it slip through my fingers. I had tested my vulnerability and fallen desperately short. I was a failure.

Many ward members tried to draw close to me and our family in the weeks and months that followed. But I wouldn't let them. The Church was better off without me. I was flawed. Like a vessel from a potter's wheel made without the proper mixture of ingredients, I might look acceptable but would crumble with ordinary use.

Within months we moved. And we didn't give a forwarding address. It was difficult for my wife and young family not to asssociate with the Church, but I insisted. I needed time to find a way for them to participate without me. I didn't want them to attend church without me, but I didn't want to go either. I didn't know how to reach a compromise. So I stalled. Give me time, I told them. Don't rush me. And so they waited. Patiently. For two and one-half years we had almost no contact with the Church. Sometimes we prayed together. Sometimes Julie would leave the *Ensign* open on the nightstand to an article on repentance and forgiveness that she hoped I would read. But I didn't. I didn't want to read about it. I didn't want to discuss it. I just wanted to leave the matter alone. I was not fit for the Lord's kingdom and neither my wife nor anyone else was going to convince me otherwise. I was not looking for sympathy, I just wanted the subject closed.

Two and one-half years after I was excommunicated, we moved into a new house in a new city. After years of living in an apartment we were finally able to own a home of our own. Within days a knock came at our door and two young men in white shirts welcomed us to the city and gave us a welcome package. We invited them in and acknowledged our familiarity with the Church. They came back several times in the next several weeks. Within two months, a home teacher was visiting us regularly.

Bob Davis was an awfully nice home teacher. Recently returned from a mission and even more recently married, he visited regularly. After a number of visits, he confronted me directly.

"Brother Nelson," he said, "you need to be back in the Church. You need to put the past behind you. We all make mistakes. We're all unworthy. So what? Why, I remember hiding some beer in the trunk of my car when I was in high school, then driving up the canyon with some of the guys to drink it."

Nice as he was, I didn't relate to Bob Davis. I knew he meant well, that he wanted to help. I just didn't think our pasts were comparable. Yet it was more than that. I knew that forgiveness followed sincere repentance. And it wasn't that I wasn't willing to repent. It was just that I honestly believed that it was in my nature to follow the ways of the world. I had been "programmed" early in life by a home and family environment that was incompatible with gospel teachings, and regardless of how hard I tried I was like an animal raised in the wilds. I could be disciplined to perform certain acts but never civilized.

Bob Davis came back a few more times, but after some months didn't return. Then, a new home teacher arrived. Henry Thompson. I didn't know he was a home teacher when he came up the walk. I didn't know who he was. Still in good health at seventy-two, Brother Thompson had seen much of the world. He had been a mission president in Europe after World War II and a stake president upon his return. After retiring five years ago, he had relocated to our city. He had served as the high priests group leader ever since.

After exchanging some pleasantries, Brother Thompson indicated that our family had been assigned to the high priests and that he had called himself to serve as our home teacher. We talked that night about what I wanted—what I expected—from him as a home teacher. I was somewhat disarmed by his patience with me, with his attempts to understand my feelings. He came back the next week. And the next. And the next. For two complete and consecutive years he visited us weekly. Sometimes we would forget about an appointment, and he would leave us a note saying he was sorry he had missed us. Sometimes we would purposely break an appointment and pass it off lightly to him during his next visit—as if we were doing *him* a favor just to meet with him. Still he came back. Every week.

Brother Thompson is not a sophisticated man. He is not a learned man. He is a simple man, self-taught. He is transparent, unable to hide his feelings and emotions be they good or bad. His weaknesses are likewise transparent, obvious to any observer. He is no man's idol. He cannot, for instance, quote the scriptures very well and frequently transposes verses. Yet he is intimately acquainted with their message and seems to be on personal terms with their author.

Brother Thompson did more than visit us weekly for two years. He came not only into our home, but also into our lives. And let us into his. He invited various ward members with him so that we would get acquainted with others. He invited us to his home for special occasions and proudly introduced us to his children and grandchildren. And he touched our hearts. Sometimes, he also touched raw nerves.

"Jim," he said to me one evening when we were alone together, "you like feeling sorry for yourself, don't you? You like 'wallering' in your own self-pity, you like telling yourself that you are a failure. You say you don't, but you do. You know why? No responsibilities. Without being responsible, you don't have to even try. You've really put yourself above everyone else; you know it? You've put yourself out of reach of anyone in the universe. You and you alone are untouchable. That's very presumptous."

I was shocked. I didn't know what to say.

"I'm afraid," I inadvertently revealed to him. "I'm afraid to try. Afraid to hurt people again. People who trusted me, people who believed in me. You would do the same thing if it were you."

I was hurt, reeling. But I had shot back, trapped him. I was ready to handle either his agreement or disagreement.

"I would forgive you even if you did," he calmly replied. "So would God. He loves you, Jim Nelson, He loves you."

I searched his face for the slightest flicker of doubt. I looked into his eyes to see if these were simple words too easily spoken. Henry Thompson is a transparent man. He did not flinch. He did not turn away. There was no masquerade. There was no place left for me to hide. I could not stop the rush of blood to my head and the flood of emotion. My free-fall flight had abruptly ended.

I started to read the scriptures again. Now I wanted to believe that there was redemption for *me*, not just for mankind, but for *me*, too. I looked at the scriptures for direction and guidance. How could I know for certain that the Lord wanted me back in His kingdom? I wanted to come back, but did He want me? Would He be better off without me? I wanted to feel acceptable to the Lord, but how?

The Book of Mormon tells of a man named Zeezrom who had argued with Alma and Amulek and had led many astray before accepting the gospel himself. Though he was converted, still he carried a heavy burden (see Alma 15:3).

He continued in this condition until he was visited by Alma, who questioned him about his faith in Christ and the plan of salvation. Although I had read this scripture before, it now carried a new meaning for me. I was like Zeezrom. I had been a stumbling block for others. But I began to have hope in my own salvation. Desperate, quiet hope. I wanted to be of some use in the Lord's kingdom. I wanted to be an asset, not a liability. But could I ever be trusted again? Could I be depended upon?

I wondered about Zeezrom. Was he a flash in the night? Did he return to his former ways? Zeezrom is mentioned only two more times in the scriptures after this incident, each time in passing. Once he is cited as accompanying Alma on a missionary journey and later he is acknowledged for bearing a powerful testimony while so engaged. He did not falter.

I was so grateful when I was allowed to be baptized again. I was not overjoyed to be rebaptized, I was relieved. I didn't feel the satisfaction of an accomplishment. It was more like the wobbly feeling that comes when a fever has passed and it's possible to get out of bed. It feels so good not to be sick anymore. It feels so good to be up and around. That's how I felt after I was baptized, that I was finally up and around.

12

What Is It Like to Be Old?

Sometimes little children will ask me what's it like to be old. They are so innocent and so unaffected by social conventions. Occasionally, a mother will overhear one of her children and, while apologizing for her child's query, will ask her child not to ask embarrassing questions. But who's embarrassed? Growing old happens to everyone. Well, practically everyone. When we think about it, most of us would probably prefer growing old to the alternative. It's amazing what a little perspective can do in such matters.

I have a friend who has a unique way of telling others what it's like to be old. He tells them to put cotton in their ears and gravel in their shoes, then pull on a pair of rubber gloves and smear some Vaseline on a pair of glasses before putting them on, and they will have it: instant aging. When my wife turned seventy-five she made an entry in her journal that described rather nicely what it feels like to be old. "I am seventy-five years old today. I never thought I'd live to see life from this view. And what a view: I can barely see, most sounds are like faint echoes, I get tired so easily, and I can hardly chew the foods I like. No eyes, no ears, no breath, no teeth. It's amazing how well a person can get along without such things."

I really do not feel like an old man inside. I still feel the same way as I did about most things when I was twenty-five. I don't know what an old man is supposed to feel like, really. I feel like the same young man I've always been, except I can't do many of the things I once could do. I thought I would *feel* differently than when I was younger, but I don't.

Our children worry about us, much more than they should. They worry about whether we can take care of ourselves. We probably can't do as well as we once did, but we get by sufficiently well.

Some bodily parts don't work as well as they once did, but that doesn't mean we can't take care of ourselves. I've had cancer of the prostrate, and blood clots, and finally had to have an entire new plumbing system installed in me; but so what? After all, I'm eighty years old. What do you expect?

That's not to say I don't become discouraged at times. I do. In fact, I'll get downright despondent and won't talk to anyone for three or four days: not to my children, not to Katie, not to the neighbors—no one. I don't know why, exactly. Mostly it's because I must depend on others for so many things. My equilibrium isn't very good. I can't always control my bowel movement. I can't see well enough to drive. I don't want to call on others for help all the time. They have their own lives to live; what do they want with an old man like me?

Sometimes I don't even think there's much worth living for. What good do I do, after all? Old people can feel useless. A friend of mine who retired when I did felt that way. His wife died, then he got cancer. All he thought he had to look forward to was a life of pain in a nursing home somewhere. So he shot himself. After his funeral, I got rid of all my guns so I wouldn't be tempted to do the same thing if things started going bad for me. Cancer has shown me that there are some things worse than dying.

But I still have Katie and as long as I do I think I'll be okay. I've told her I want to die first so that I won't have to be here without her, alone. I can see what things are like on the other side that way, too. I've been a carpenter by trade and I want to be certain there's a fitting house for her. But I'll probably need her to pick up my socks over there, too, so she had better not stay here too long after I go.

Probably the worst aspect of growing old is not having children around. Didn't expect that from an old codger like me, did you? But it's true. I saw a lady at the grocery store recently with a small baby in the grocery cart. I went up to her, tapped her on the shoulder, and pointing to the baby, said, "Excuse me, ma'am, on what shelf can I get one of those?"

I've always loved children. All ages. All colors. The giant economy size, the small convenient size, and everything in between. Maybe it comes from working in the old Mutual program for so many years or being bishop for nearly a decade. Maybe it comes from raising four of my own. And forty-three foster children who are just like my own. Or maybe it's because my wife and I were camp directors every summer for twenty-three years for the region girls' camp. Twenty-three years is a long time to do anything. Know how many different girls stayed there at least a week in the twenty-three years? Seventeen thousand. We told stories to, washed dishes with, planned skits for, and hiked up mountains alongside seventeen thousand girls. I've got their names all on a roster I can show you if you want to see them.

I have lots of good memories. Most of my life is over, I know that. I can look back with satisfaction, but I can also look forward with anticipation. There are things I want to do. I have a little trailer by a lake and am building a summer cabin there. My sons are helping me do it. We don't make much progress when they come to help me, which is frustrating to them, but just the way I want it. You see, they want us to have a nice place, and I know I can't work much on it by myself. So as long as there are things which need to be done, I can count on them to visit us and work on them. So I'd be surprised if we ever finish it. Certainly, it is one of my goals to never complete it. I enjoy the extra company I get too much.

Sometimes younger people think that those who are elderly are only living in the past. They hear us talk about memorable times and think that we do not have goals or things that we want to do. I think it is a common misconception. I have lots of goals left. *Not* finishing our cabin is just one of them. Visiting with family and friends is another. So is keeping our family home evening group going. There are ten of us, mostly older couples, who've met nearly every week since the Church started printing family home evening manuals. We usually use the scriptures instead of the manuals, however. They seem more pertinent for us. Most of us in the group are preparing for our final exams so we need different lessons. So I do have goals. And wishes, too. Mainly, I wish I could see my children, grandchildren, and great-grandchildren more often. I want to tell them about things which are important to me. I want them all to have lots of children so they will bring them by to show me and stay for a while to visit. I don't want to be a stranger to them. I want to be Grandpa.

I guess all of our wishes can't be fulfilled just the way that we want them. It's nice to have wishes. Wishing helps me a lot some days. I think it's kinder to acknowledge a wish while noting its impossibility than it is to deny it altogether. "Yes, I know, I wish so, too" doesn't hurt anybody and is more supportive than "You can't, so there's no use wishing." Even though I can't have my daughter and her family as nearby as I would like, wishing helps to keep me forward-looking instead of living in the past. I don't know why people think they have to dash old people's optimism by telling them not to wish for things. Nobody feels they must tell a boy or girl of average ability they won't be a major league ball player or a Supreme Court justice. Why must we insist on pouring cold water on elderly folks' wishes?

Sometimes my wishing turns to worrying. Old people are entitled to worry. They've spent their entire lives doing it and they've got to fill the space with something. We get too tired too easily to do all we want to do so we use worry to fill up the space. It doesn't do any good, I know (after all, I wasn't born yesterday), but it does fill up the space. I worry mainly about two things: what will happen to me if I can't take care of myself, and will the Lord think that I've lived a good enough life to "make it."

I am glad that I can still take care of myself. Being dependent on someone else for everything is a great indignity. No wonder older people are short-tempered—"crotchety." I would be too if I couldn't take care of myself. Imagine it! It makes me shudder just to think about it! But it could happen to me, I realize. I may be older, but I'm not naive.

Katie and I have lived for forty-five years right here in this same house. I never did like to move. It feels good to live in our own home. It is a comfort to me which I don't want to give up unless I absolutely must. I told a young friend when Katie and I celebrated our golden wedding anniversary that we live by some simple rules which enable us to get along quite well despite our advancing age. If the toothbrush is wet, then we have already brushed our teeth. If the clock-radio that serves as our alarm is hot on top, then we left it on all night. If I am wearing one black and one brown shoe, then I'm quite certain there is a matching pair in the closet. With such simple rules as these, it's quite easy to cope with the occasional forgetfulness and ordinariness of advancing age.

What would I do if I couldn't take care of myself? I hope I could talk to my children about it. I certainly wouldn't want them to make a decision to take me out of my home without my consent. I've thought about what I would do if I couldn't continue to live by myself and talked with my children about it once. I think it was healthy to talk about it although we didn't resolve everything. It was reassuring to talk about such things and see their perspectives. One of my daughters did some reading and found out that about 12 or 13 percent of all elderly will end up moving in with their children, which is about the same number who will spend some time in nursing homes. The rest—about 75 percent, which is certainly the majority—remain in their own homes and pass away while living there. I certainly hope I'll be in that number.

I want to be in another number, too. The number who are granted permission to return to live with our Father in Heaven. Death is no longer a remote possibility. Will I be ready when it happens? Some days I think that surely the Lord will overlook my imperfections as minor. Other days, I recognize that He "cannot look upon sin with the least degree of allowance." I feel like Tevye in *Fiddler on the Roof,* who was continually looking at things in a certain way, only to consider that "on the other hand" there might be another way to look at a situation. It seems that I, also, have two hands and have difficulty weighing and passing judgment on my own worthiness.

I think that living alone in old age causes a person to come to terms with himself more than any other experience. Old age is an intense and varied experience, not the long defeat toward the inevitable that some would make it. Some days, when I am feeling poorly, I whisper to myself, "Am I dying? Is this how my life will finally end?" So far the answer has always been, "No, not yet. You're not giving up are you?" I'm not a Pollyanna, but I do try to search for a positive meaning in the experiences that I have.

The myth of old age characterized chiefly as a disabling era of life, a sad ending to a life well lived, is simply inaccurate. Old age is not an illness, it is a timeless ascent. As our physical stamina diminishes, our ability to see things in perspective grows. As long as people don't think of growing old as "the end," they will still be greedy to live their lives to the fullest. Those who think of retirement or growing older as coming to the end of a journey won't like it. They probably won't spend much time in it either because they will probably die sooner. I think of old age as simply another era with its own mountains to climb. I'm probably less concerned about arriving anywhere in particular than when I was younger, although I do want to make progress. I rest more along the path than I once did. But I'm not lying along the roadside. I'll manage.

I've always managed. I've managed to make it through some hard times before—two World Wars, the Great Depression, lots of kids. I'll manage now, too. Old age cannot take away my identity. I know who I am, what I've been. And I'm not through yet.

13

Going Home

I used to avoid talking about painful topics. Life is full of so much goodness and joy, why dwell on the negative? Why worry about things which may never happen? I shrink from even thinking about some of life's inevitable trials: growing old, the death of my husband or a child. I don't even like to visit friends who are hospitalized. What if that were me? What would I do? When I hear about those who experience difficult trials, I sometimes offer a silent prayer to the Lord for the affected family—and for myself. "I'll do almost anything, but please don't give me *that* experience." Instantly I realize the Lord will try each of us in ways that will test our devotion and commitment. And so I attempt to block out my silent prayers and thoughts, as if not thinking about painful events will somehow provide me with insurance that they won't happen to me. Since my husband is a seminary teacher, I expect that the Lord will take his commitment to full-time gospel service as an affirmation of our testimonies and allow us to live our tranquil lives. I don't really want the character strengthening which comes from difficulties. I want to live a predictable, uneventful, ordinary life.

I don't remember thinking about these things when I was taken into the delivery room to give birth to our little child. I was apprehensive, but under the circumstances I thought that was normal. It had been a difficult pregnancy, and I had prayed that having this child later than the normal childbearing years would be a blessing to our family. I had some foreboding—would this child be born normal, without any mental or physical handicaps?—but I passed my feelings off as typical jitters. I had felt the same way on the four previous trips to the hospital. Everything would be fine. In a few hours the delivery would be all over. In a few days we would be back at home with a new baby. Nothing to worry about.

I try not to remember the pain of giving birth to a new baby. It is appropriately called labor. It is hard work. Finally, he came. At 2:25 A.M., Gregory Stephen Johnson entered the world. Finally.

It is such a relief to hold a new baby after giving birth. So comforting. So reassuring. Like the coming of spring, a baby's birth signals hope and optimism. Things will get better. But everything was not all right with our little new-born. At first the doctors thought his heart just needed a little time and a little help to pump the blood through his body. But five days later, they sent us home with downcast eyes. Our little boy had an inoperable heart condition. He would die before the week was over. "Take him home," they said. "Hold him and love him as much as you can."

And love him we did. Everyone in our family—children, cousins. Neighbors. He was so alert but seemed in such pain. He was difficult to comfort, to console. He would cuddle so easily to me, however, and look deeply into my eyes. Oh, how I loved this little boy, this child of mine.

I prayed fervently that he might live. I felt such a bond with this little boy. He seemed to know me so well, not just as his mother, but as a person. I resolved that my faith was going to be complete, unwavering, nothing doubting. I did not think that I had asked Heavenly Father for anything much out of the ordinary in my life. My needs had been simple. Now I needed His help. I would ask, expecting to receive; seek, expecting to find; knock, expecting it would be opened unto me.

Day after day, I watched our young son slowly die. Seven days after his birth, my pediatrician marveled that he was still alive. But he was so weak and limp in my arms and cried with such pain. My desperate hope seemed taxed to the limit. A friend often visited to comfort me and help with the house and other children. She encouraged me to take this event in stride and adopt an eternal perspective. "Just think," she once said, "you'll have a child waiting for you on the other side of the veil who is promised celestial glory. What an incentive!" Though she meant well, her words were not very comforting. I wanted my baby *now*. I didn't want to wait.

Another week passed. The doctors were amazed. It was a miracle our baby was still alive, they said. Could their initial diagnosis have been wrong? Or had our prayers softened the Lord's heart and He, in turn, healed our son? We did not know. More tests were conducted, but the answer was still the same. His condition had not changed; for some reason he was still alive. But why? What was the reason?

I searched the scriptures for guidance. Perhaps I wasn't doing everything quite right. Perhaps the Lord was waiting to bless us, had kept Gregory alive until we could find the missing equation in a formula that would allow Him to intervene and perform a miracle in our lives. But what was it? I searched frantically, desperately. What was I missing? What was I overlooking? "Oh, please, dear Father in Heaven, show me what I must do." I read and reread each of the Savior's miracles while in His earthly ministry. There had to be a clue there, but where? I looked again and again at these passages from the scriptures. I didn't know what else to do. I tried to do everything I could. And hoped.

Spring shaped the outside world as another week passed. Gregory was eating better, more active, more alert. He seemed to get stronger every day. He'd done so much better and breathed quite easily now. We visited another doctor. He couldn't explain Gregory's condition. "Maybe he'll make it," he suggested. "Maybe his body will adapt to the condition of his heart. He will probably never be able to do all the things other children do, but maybe he'll make it. *Maybe*."

Weeks passed. At times he seemed so healthy and alert, at other times so listless and tired. When he would toss and turn or cry out at night, I would pick him up and rock him and everything would seem to be all right again. I would pray at such times that Gregory might relax and sleep, and almost simultaneously he would drift off. I knew that my Heavenly Father heard and answered my prayers. I knew it was as simple a matter for the Lord to give my child life as it was to let him relax and sleep.

Though sleep often came, relief did not. Good days came less and less often, bad days lingered and seemed to run together continuously. Some evenings we would pick up an odd-seeming, stiff, grotesque little body, his head thrown back and his back arched. His last breath seemed so near. We said our good-byes and cried and dreamed about futures we wished we could have. Our emotions had been on a roller coaster as we went from hope to despair and back to hope again. Finally, we asked the Lord to release his spirit from his body. Our hope and despair had turned to acceptance. Release him, we prayed. We do not wish to see this innocent child suffer so.

But he did not go. Day after day we watched and held and prayed for Gregory. Still he lingered, often seemingly comatose. The doctors recommended that we begin giving him morphine for the pain. *Morphine!* Our sweet baby, barely alive, given morphine? Reluctantly, we consented. We had clung to a glimmer of hope until now; when we decided to give this painkiller to our little one, there was no hope left.

Still, Gregory Stephen clung to life. Emaciated, often gasping for breath, he would not give up on life. Why? Why would God not take him? What purpose was being served? We had accepted the inevitable; why not release him and let him return to his heavenly home? Why torture this little child of mine? But nothing changed. So I wrote in my journal.

> God is mean and hurtful and I don't like Him anymore. He is so mean to me. He just keeps hurting me and hurting me and He won't stop. I've tried so hard to be faithful and obey and to follow, and He just keeps hurting me every day. He's a mean Father and I don't want to be His friend because He's so mean and hurtful. I can't stand any more hurt, but if He doesn't love me and wants to hurt me, I'll guess I'll just have to take it. What else can I do? But I won't ask Him to help me anymore.

Day after day he suffered, sometimes passing blood, sometimes lying still on a blanket, sometimes struggling for breath. Late one afternoon he cried out while I was holding him, and I bent over putting my lips to his ear. "Go, my son," I said. "Go now when you have the chance. Don't worry about me. You don't have to take care of me any more. Leave this body. You're not leaving us alone; you've helped blaze a trail and the path is clearer now. The mist is clearer, the iron rod more secure, the goal more visible. Go, Greg, go.''

He relaxed, then gasped several times. Then shuddered. He was gone.

I lifted up my eyes to God. I had tried to turn my back on Him and not go to Him anymore. I had tried to go it alone. I didn't want to rely on anyone else anymore. I was hurt and disappointed and afraid. But I couldn't turn my back on God. Even when it seemed He didn't hear or answer, how could I leave Him? I didn't have anywhere else to go. Was He mean, cruel? Who had given me this precious gift of a child in the first place? Was it somehow my right to demand and receive exactly what I wanted just the way I wanted? A child at a candy store may have such wishes; should I? But why the pain, the suffering? It seems so senseless, so unnecessary.

I don't believe there are answers to such questions which can be ladled from a universal bucket of wisdom. A measure of the quality of our spiritual life is our ability to develop *personal* answers to what are ultimately very personal concerns. Did Gregory have to die? Was it his time? Did he need only a short time on earth? Was this a test of my faith, a means of determining my ability to say ''Thy will be done?'' Or was there simply a natural law of genetics that was broken somewhere along the way while his tiny little body was being formed? Was his short life just one of those accidents that come from living in an imperfect world?

I believe the answers to such questions differ from situation to situation. There are no universally applicable responses, only individual ones for specific situations. But there are answers. God does not require us to wonder or to worry if we seek His advice.

The death of a loved one is rarely easy to bear. I consider this experience a pivotal point in my life. I know that life is a mixture of the bitter and the sweet and now I realize that I have only so much control over the events that will impact my life. Some things I can change, others I must accept. Though I would gladly exchange the serenity and perspective I've gained to have my son back, I have learned much. It provided me with a situation in which trusting in God became a necessity. God is not an indifferent bystander; He does intervene.

I no longer avoid hospitals. I seek them out knowing that their occupants need guidance and are likely fearful about their capacity to meet the demands of their particular crisis. Nor do I avoid talking about painful events in the lives of others as I once did. Sometimes I still offer a silent prayer, quietly requesting to be spared a particular adversity that someone else has had to come to terms with. But not as often.

I worry less, too. Not that I think that I have satisfied my quota for difficult experiences—rather, I know myself better. I know that the Lord will not turn His back on me regardless of my hurt or anger. I can always go Home.

14

Facing Problems Without Losing Faith

Difficulties, problems, and crises beset all of us. Some come early in life, some come later. Some come and stay like an unwanted guest that we don't know how to ask to leave. Some come almost unnoticed and go away just as quietly. Regardless of how or when they come, they do come. We are not overlooked. Nor are we ignored simply because we are faithful Latter-day Saints.

Elder S. Dilworth Young, a member of the First Quorum of the Seventy until his death, was very familiar with the power of the priesthood and the miracles wrought in lives of faithful Latter-day Saints. He had seen people surmount difficulties, overcome problems, and weather many storms through the Lord's assistance. He had given blessings which restored health to the ill and provided counsel and inspiration to the weary. So when World War II began and his beloved son was called into the military service, he prepared to give him a father's blessing that he would safely return home. Elder Young and his son climbed to the top of Mount Ben Lomond, one of the tallest peaks in Utah. There they prayed together, under the heavens, close to God. There he laid his hands upon his son's head to bless him that he would return home safely. But the words would not come. He was left alone on that outdoor balcony to speak sacred words of instruction without a blessing of promised protection. They walked home together, father and son, each knowing that the purpose of their journey was not fulfilled in the way they intended. The father returned to his work, while the son went to a war from which he would not return. Dilworth R. Young was killed in action in 1943.

Miracles occur, we know that. When we lose loved ones or do not receive the blessings we believe we are entitled to, we may be troubled by the faith-promoting experiences of those who have been miraculously spared. We read that "the effectual fervent prayer of a righteous man availeth much" (James 5:16). Are we to conclude that our prayers are somehow not as effective as those of others who were miraculously protected or otherwise blessed?

President Joseph F. Smith indicated this was not the case. "Many things occur in the world in which it seems very difficult for most of us to find a solid reason for the acknowledgement of the hand of the Lord. I have come to the belief that the only reason I have been able to discover by which we should acknowledge the hand of God in some occurrences is the fact that the thing which has occurred has been permitted of the Lord." (*Gospel Doctrine*, 5th ed. [Salt Lake City: Deseret Book Company, 1939], p. 56.)

In other words, a trial may not be the will of the Lord, but it occurs with His permission. He will not constantly intervene to alter events, because to do so would diminish our agency. Yet He is ever available to comfort and assist us to cope with any difficulty. He cannot make the world safe for us, but He can enable us to deal constructively with any difficulty. He will teach us, comfort us, succor us, heal us. But we must also do our part. We cannot suppose that strength and guidance will be given to us simply for the asking. Just as Oliver Cowdery was expected to study things out in his own mind and then ask the Lord if his judgment was correct in attempting to translate the Book of Mormon (see D&C 9:7–9), so we must do our part in coping with life's difficulties and challenges. How? What are the common experiences of those who come to terms with trials and difficulties and go on to live life to the fullest? How do they do it?

Share Your Burden

We are meant to help each other. When we independently assume we can work things out by ourselves we not only shut off potential sources of help, but we may also become self-centered. Talking about difficulties helps us to see our situations more clearly and less one-sidedly. People who are experiencing a crisis or are trying to work through a particular trial in their lives simply need to get some "distance" from it—to take a step back and integrate it into a broad view of life's purposes and potential. Life is sometimes very hard. We should not minimize its difficulties.

On our own, we may be too close to a problem to see it for what it is or to see alternate ways of responding to it. Typically when we experience a crisis, we hold a magnifying glass up to it—and to ourselves—to try to understand what is going on and why. While magnifying enlarges things, it also shows them out of proportion. We often need some distance in time or events to gain a better perspective. By sharing our burdens, our concerns, our frustrations with someone else, we are more likely to gain insights into our personal motivations, including what we value and how we define success for ourselves. Such insights do not come easily, but they are worth the effort.

Too often in coping with an emotional crisis, we worry about how we *should* feel and cover up how we *do* feel. Simply ventilating our feelings is not sufficient, of course, until we act on those feelings and make some decisions about what course of action to pursue. However, by examining our feelings in minute detail—going beyond expressing them openly—we are able to see them for what they are: grief, frustration, sadness, anger, guilt, disappointment, fear. This puts them in perspective and increases our ability to deal with them positively. We can't always change events, but we can control our reactions to them.

People who are able to overcome the cynicism or bitterness or disappointment (often the initial reaction to a personal trial or difficulty) say that the help of a friend is essential, a friend who doesn't judge or condemn them for having negative thoughts or feelings, but likewise does not passively allow such reactions to be continuously repeated. Such friends, instead, expose their own vulnerabilities, their own inadequacies, their own misgivings, and having done so become partners in trying to sort out where life's journey goes next. They are available, concerned, and caring.

Talk to the Lord

The Lord is also available to listen and comfort us—not in some abstract way, but in very personal and individual ways. We can discuss our hurt or frustration or disappointment with Him! We have the right to His comfort, His influence, to have Him "speak peace to [our] mind concerning the matter" (D&C 6:23).

If we have a close relationship with someone, in that person's company we don't worry about showing anger, frustration, or other healthy emotions, subject to normal restraints. We don't mind saying what we think. By social custom we show restraint with strangers, not explaining our actions to them or expecting them to explain theirs to us. But with our spouses, our children, our closest friends it is not so—we want to know why they do things as they do, and we get straight to the point about it. Do we regard the Lord as a stranger or as a family member? Do we seek explanations from Him (if in His wisdom He finds it appropriate to explain), or are we simply polite and reserved with Him? When Joseph Smith felt alone and abandoned in Liberty Jail, he poured out his feelings to a God who would not be offended by expressed hurt and frustration. Because they were not strangers, Joseph could say what he thought and know that the Lord would sift the wheat from the chaff in his words. Note the Prophet's words:

> O God, where art thou? And where is the pavilion that covereth thy hiding place?
>
> How long shall thy hand be stayed, and thine eye, yea thy pure eye, behold from the eternal heavens the wrongs of thy people and of thy servants, and thine ear be penetrated with their cries?
>
> Yea, O Lord, how long shall they suffer these wrongs and unlawful oppressions, before thine heart shall be softened toward them, and thy bowels be moved with compassion toward them? (D&C 121:1–3.)

We would never talk like that to a stranger. If we can communicate to God, He will listen and not leave us comfortless. He can even heal a broken heart.

Say Good-bye, Look Ahead

Divorce, unemployment, growing old, death—all these involve a personal loss: loss of a companion, loss of income, loss of opportunity, loss of a loved one. We are continually leaving some aspects of our lives and going on to others. Sometimes our leave-taking may be planned: moving, retirement, marriage of the last child at home. Often it is unplanned and unexpected.

In such circumstances, we may not know when—or even how—to say good-bye. In not wanting to give up good memories, we may cling to the past. When a child dies a mother grieves for her little one. But she has also lost her *role* as a mother in addition to her loss of a child. We become attached to habits and routines just as we do to people. When the meaning is taken from the routine, we don't know what to do. We are bewildered. "What do I do now?" We cannot rely on the old routine to keep us going because it too is changed, different, gone. This is true of other changes which may occur in our lives as well, not just the death of a loved one. If a marriage breaks up, or we lose a job, or must move to another location, things change for us. We must say good-bye to the old and turn to the new.

Too often people who have experienced a personal loss return to their old routine and try to "get over" their longing as quickly as possible. They may even try to quickly restore their loss by turning to a suitable replacement. But sadness and grief, mourning and longing, are natural and necessary responses to losses. They are positive reactions because they focus on reality, on what is really happening. They must be given their place, they must have their day. But their bounds must also be set. We can ourselves decide the length of their stay, their place in our lives. Instead of looking immediately for substitutes, we must give losses their due before going on. We must say, "I wish this were not so, but it is. I'll not deny that I wish things were different, but I'll not grieve forever. I'll choose an alternative route to my goal of happiness and fulfillment and go on from here." Some pain, some loneliness may persist, but those feelings can be a lantern to illuminate the future. By not trying to forget the past, we avoid denying what has happened. By planning for the future, we are more likely to get on with our lives.

Rebuilding

As we go through life we aspire to many things—recognition in our jobs, a happy family life, new experiences, church service. And we often ask ourselves, "Should I want to do that? What right do I have to seek that goal?" Losses, difficulties, trials, and problems make us especially self-critical. We doubt our capacity to go on, to inherit eternal blessings that the Lord holds out to each of us. We may say, "If I can't even get what I want here, what right do I have to expect that things will be any different hereafter?" We are particularly vulnerable to such self-doubts in the midst of personal crises.

We can aid the process of rebuilding by introspectively examining our abilities and capabilities—what we enjoy doing and are able to do well. It might even be well to discuss answers to the following questions with a friend or loved one to help the process along:

1. What do you like to do? When you are feeling good about yourself, what things are you doing?

2. What have been the half-dozen most gratifying experiences in your life? The joy you had in the experience was really the joy you have in yourself. What were you doing?

3. Who are and were your role models, your heroes or heroines? Think about relatives, friends, teachers, characters in scripture. What did they say or do that caused you to admire them?

4. What decisions have you made that you feel good about? What major life choices have you been glad you made?

5. What aspects of your life do you enjoy now? Is what you are doing helping you? Noticing what you are doing now is important because what we do influences profoundly what we think and how we feel. For example, if you sit home alone all day feeling miserable and thinking unhappy thoughts, you can

more directly change your sitting around than you can your miserable feelings and despondent thoughts. So change them! When you start to move around and become more productive, you will feel less depressed, because depression feeds on inaction and feelings of inadequacy.

6. What are you going to do next? What plans are you going to make for the future? Without plans we are like ships without rudders. Over and over we should continually try to figure out a better way to make the most of the future.

Conclusion

Difficulties are a part of life. We know that. We see it all around us. But regardless of how prepared we are when personal trials come our way, they still hurt. We may want to retreat, to go backward instead of forward. We may feel alone, set adrift to fend for ourselves. We want everything the same for everyone; "It's only fair that it be that way," we tell ourselves, and we may become embittered when things don't seem "fair." But the routes to eternal life vary for all of us. Some appear easier and others more difficult. The terrain for some appears smooth and well-paved, while for others it is broken and rough. We do not always know why.

In a memorial service conducted for military servicemen, President Harold B. Lee offered this perspective in quoting Albert Schweitzer:

Don't vex your mind trying to explain the suffering you have to endure in this life. Don't think that God is punishing you or disciplining you or rejecting you. Even in the midst of suffering you are in His Kingdom. You are always His child and He has His protecting arms around you. Does a child understand everything his father does?

No, but he can confidently nestle in his father's arms and feel perfect happiness, even while tears glisten in his eyes, because he is his father's child. (As quoted in *From the Valley of Despair to the Mountain Peaks of Hope* [pamphlet, 1971], pp. 11–12.)

In quiet moments of reflection we realize that our journey is not for this life alone. Some who seem to have found a comfortable way station are, in fact, being distracted from pressing on to an eternal destination by the conveniences of the moment. Sometimes, it appears those things which make us the most competitive in this life distract us from nobler goals.

And if we weather our storms well, then what?

If we are patient, our Father will heal even a broken heart, the same broken heart and contrite spirit that provide exclusive passage into the kingdom of God. Our routes may vary, but there is one gate through which all must enter.